SKINNY
SOUPS

SKINNY SOUPS

80 flavor-packed recipes of less than 300 calories

Kathryn Bruton

Photography by Laura Edwards

Kyle Books

To Dad

Published in 2017 by Kyle Books
www.kylebooks.com

Distributed by National Book Network
4501 Forbes Blvd, Suite 200,
Lanham, MD 20706
Phone: (800) 462-6420
Fax: (800) 338-4550
customercare@nbnbooks.com

First published in Great Britain in 2016 by
Kyle Books, an imprint of Kyle Cathie Ltd.

10 9 8 7 6 5 4 3 2 1

ISBN 978-1-909487-50-5

Project Editor: Claire Rogers
Copy Editor: Anne Newman
Americanizer: Christy Lusiak
Designer: Louise Leffler
Photographer: Laura Edwards
Food Stylists: Annie Rigg and Kathryn Bruton
Prop Stylist: Liz Belton
Production: Nic Jones and Gemma John

Library of Congress Control Number: 2016946904

Color reproduction by F1, London
Printed and bound in China by 1010 International
Printing Ltd.

Nutritional information key:
DF—dairy-free
GF—gluten-free
V—vegetarian
VE—vegan

contents

introduction

I adore soup. It is the simplest of concepts with endless potential. Every culture has its own version, each as interesting and inspiring as the next. There is no limit to how healthy a soup can be and the recipes in this book showcase how it can be exciting and different, bursting with fantastic ingredients, flavors, and textures, low in calories, and high in nutrients—all at the same time. It is the epitome of food for mind, body, and soul.

Everyone can make soup successfully. As with anything homemade, you can pack it with goodness. As well as being full of healthy ingredients, every recipe in this book is less than 300 calories per portion, and many are even less. No calorie-controlled meal should leave you hungry. Here you will find soups fit for a main meal, fantastically filling lunch options, breakfast bowls designed to positively kick-start your day, and even delicious desserts, a testament to how creative this wonderful dish can be.

I love to play around with ideas, be creative, and design imaginative and original dishes—you won't find any leek and potato soups in this book. Instead, I have used my imagination to create delicious, interesting recipes. The quest to pack each bowl with goodness and flavor is the backbone of each recipe, and I hope that you will feel inspired to cook soup bursting with flavors you either love or are interested to try.

This book is for everyone—those with and without food intolerances and those who eliminate certain food groups from their diet. Soups are often, by default, vegetarian, vegan, or gluten- or dairy-free, and many of the recipes in this book are some, if not all, of the above. Where they are not, a few simple changes will make them suitable for you in most cases.

The chapters have been organized to showcase soup's adaptability. Creamy creations make their way into the Smooth Soups chapter, some served simply, others adorned with exciting garnishes. My travels around Southeast Asia inspired many of the recipes in the Broths and Consommés chapter. The 15-Minute Soups chapter will hopefully help when you are constantly chasing your tail. Grains and Pulses take center stage in their very own chapter, and the last chapter champions superfoods for a concentrated dose of nutrition.

Creating the recipes in this book has been one of my most interesting and exciting adventures— many happy months were spent consuming and being all-consumed by soup. I could go on forever; such is the versatility of this humble dish—it has infinite possibilities. My adventure is finished and, in buying this book, you have begun yours. Every recipe is open to interpretation, ready for you to stamp with your personality, if you so wish. Whether you use these recipes as guide to eat healthier, aid weight loss, or simply enjoy some delicious bowls, the only thing I ask is that you have fun doing it.

equipment

The beauty of soup is that it requires very little kitchen equipment and much of what you need will most likely be in your cupboards already. However, there are a few pieces that are particularly useful, and it may be worth investing in some of the items below to achieve the best possible results.

Blenders, hand-held immersion blenders, and food processors

A blended soup is at its best when it is smooth like velvet. Specifically designed to deal with liquids, a blender gives soups a beautifully smooth and uniform consistency and is my weapon of choice. If you are planning to make a lot of soup, I would recommend investing in one of these.

A hand-held immersion blender will also do the trick, although some vegetables such as broccoli, cauliflower, and corn resist the smaller, less powerful blade, resulting in a somewhat grainy texture. If you already have an immersion blender and would rather not invest in another piece of kitchen equipment, you can try passing the soup through a strainer after blending for a smoother consistency.

Food processors pose much the same problem, only in this case the blade is too big and clunky. I also find that the soup can overflow, creating a real mess. To avoid this, try blending in batches and, again, pass through a strainer afterward if necessary.

Strainer and muslin cloth

A large strainer or sieve is a hugely useful piece of equipment and will be called on many times throughout this book. Muslin cloth can be found online and in specialty cooking stores. It is inexpensive and can be washed and reused if desired. Cheesecloth will also suffice.

Mortar and pestle

This is extremely useful for making pestos and pastes and will be called for in quite a few recipes. A mini food processor will work if you don't have one.

Saucepans and baking sheets

A couple of good-quality medium size saucepans and an ovenproof casserole dish or Dutch oven will see you through almost all of the recipes in this book. I would also recommend investing in a large stockpot if you don't already have one. A couple of baking sheets will come in handy for roasting vegetables too.

Ice cube trays

Fridge and freezer space can often be scarce, so I have included instructions for making homemade stock into frozen cubes on page 16. Coconut milk is often used in small quantities throughout the book, so I would recommend opening a can and freezing tablespoon measures in an ice cube tray to avoid waste.

Plastic containers and labels

The majority of the recipes in this book are designed to serve four. If you are cooking for fewer people, the soup will keep in the fridge or freezer in most cases. Plastic containers are extremely useful for storing leftover soup, and I always label containers with the name of the soup, as well as the date it was made. Empty yogurt or butter tubs, takeout containers, or even some plastic bottles are also good for storage.

Mandolin

This is a fantastic tool for thinly slicing vegetables, and extremely useful for making Vegetable Chips (pages 45–47).

Digital weighing scales

An essential piece of equipment.

The basics

A good set of sharp knives is needed, as lots of chopping is to be done. A blunt knife is much more dangerous than a sharp one, as it can slip when chopping, so keep them sharp. A few wooden spoons, spatulas, a good-quality vegetable peeler, and a ladle will also be used continually.

a few useful notes

Seasoning

I always use sea salt and freshly cracked black pepper. In most cases I don't give quantities; if you are unsure, add a little at first and build up until it is right for you.

Low-fat vs full-fat

I tend to eat and cook ingredients in their most natural form, so, with the exception of 1% milk, you won't find any low-fat versions here. I would happily consume less of something natural than more of something that has been processed. At least that way, I know what I'm eating!

Freezing and defrosting

Almost all of the soups here are suitable for freezing (those that are not are highlighted). I like to freeze my soup in either one- or two-person portions. If you are organized, defrost them in the fridge overnight. Otherwise, place the soup container in hot water to quickly defrost the soup. If you are in a rush, do this for long enough to allow you to remove the frozen soup from the container, then gently reheat.

Ingredients

Using fresh ingredients is key to success, making a noticeable difference to the final flavor of your soup. Keep an eye on what you have in your fridge, and try to use ingredients before they are past the point of no return. Although soup is a great way to use things up, if a vegetable has a funky smell, this is likely to transfer to your soup.

Recipes

I cannot emphasize enough the importance of reading a recipe through, at least once, if not twice, and having everything you need ready before you start. Throughout the book there are many instructions in the ingredients lists, so placed to encourage you to do this preparation before you move on to cooking. Preparation makes for a happy and, more importantly, successful cook! Remember, recipes are but a guideline and are open to interpretation—don't be afraid to add your own twists and experiment with ideas.

Ground spices

A fantastic pantry addition for their long shelf life. However, nothing lasts forever and the flavor and intensity will start to deplete over time. If you haven't used a jar of ground spices in 6 months, it's time to invest in a fresh one.

Intolerances and special diets

Many of the recipes in this book are gluten- and dairy-free, vegan, and vegetarian. Where they are not, it is often very simple to alter them with a few subtle changes.

Herbs

Herbs add a punchy or delicate flavor to all kinds of dishes and recipes, and my fridge is never without them. To get the most life from your herbs, wrap them in paper towels, dampen with cold water, and refrigerate. Repeat every couple of days for a fridge life of about a week.

pantry suggestions

The list below won't cover you for every recipe, but includes many that are used more than once or that are helpful to have on hand. Many of the Asian ingredients are easy to find online, so I have included those I feel are the best ones to purchase based on their shelf life and how often they are used.

Basic pantry

Sea salt and black peppercorns
Oil—canola, olive, and toasted sesame
Tomato paste and chopped tomatoes
Pomegranate molasses
Dried wild mushrooms
Good-quality roasted red bell peppers
(preserved in water and vinegar, not oil)
Star anise
Cinnamon sticks and ground cinnamon
Ground turmeric
Cumin (seeds and ground)
Coriander (seeds and ground)
Chile flakes
Frozen peas
Canned chickpeas
Black glutinous rice
Wild rice
Black quinoa
Red and yellow split lentils
Rye flour

Baking soda
Soft-pitted prunes
Seeds—pumpkin, chia, and flaxseeds
Walnuts
Jumbo oats

Asian

Coconut oil
Miso paste (barley and sweet miso used often)
Bonito flakes
Kombu
Black sesame seeds
Fish sauce
Soy sauce (or tamari if cooking gluten-free)
Kimchi
Tofu
Mirin
Gochujang
Edamame (keep in freezer)
Wonton wrappers

unusual ingredients

There are some ingredients throughout the book that may be unfamiliar. Below is a breakdown of some of the more unusual ones and where you might find them (see also Suppliers on page 156).

Black sesame seeds

White sesame seeds are easier to come by, but I favor black for their crunchier texture and more intense flavor. You can find them in health food stores and online.

Black quinoa

This gluten-free pseudo "grain" is a complete protein and is, in fact, a seed. You can get white, red, and black quinoa, but I prefer the nuttier, sweeter taste of the black variety. You will find it in supermarkets and health food stores. If you can't find black, use white or red.

Coconut oil

Always invest in organic virgin coconut oil for cooking. At room temperature it is solid, but quickly melts when it hits the heat.

Coconut water

This gives a delicate coconut flavor and mild sweetness to broths and stock bases. Look for unsweetened pure coconut water.

Edamame

Green like peas, with a more oval shape and a delicious crunchy texture, edamame are young soybeans high in protein and fiber.

They are great in soups, as a snack, and in salads. You can buy them in the freezer section in supermarkets, Asian stores, or online.

Gochujang

This punchy Korean chile paste is wonderfully versatile and can be used in soups, stews, salad dressings, and marinades. Once opened, store in the fridge. It can be found in Asian supermarkets or online.

Konnyaki shirataki noodles

These zero-calorie noodles hail from Japan and are a good source of dietary fiber. Alone they are almost tasteless, but they take on the flavors of whatever they are cooked with. Some big supermarkets stock these, but you are most likely to find them online.

Miso

Miso is made from fermented soybeans or grains and comes in many varieties. It has a wonderful, intense flavor and is packed with all kinds of good bacteria and antioxidants. If you have a gluten intolerance, be sure to use one that is gluten-free. Lots of supermarkets stock miso pastes now, but I always buy mine online or in Asian grocery stores for variety and quality.

Nori

Thin sheets of dried seaweed and full of umami flavor, nori is used in this book as a garnish, almost like a seasoning. You will find it in the Asian section of your supermarket. Once opened, store in an airtight container or wrap tightly in plastic wrap.

Pomegranate molasses

Found in most supermarkets, this is the concentrated juice of pomegranates. It is a powerful ingredient, intensely sweet and sour. A little goes a long way, and it can create amazing, contrasting flavors.

Soy sauce

Soy sauce is a versatile ingredient in soup-making, acting as a seasoning or a stock base and giving instant depth of flavor. Go for high-quality brands, and get to know the varieties. Some will be saltier, some more intense. Kikkoman is my favorite. If you are gluten intolerant, use tamari, but be aware that it can be stronger in flavor.

Soy, almond, and hazelnut milks

Unsweetened soy and nut milks are naturally low in calories and fat. They are a great source of vitamins and minerals and boast their own unique flavor. I use them in recipes that benefit from a creamy finish. They are easy to make at home by soaking raw nuts, blending, and then straining. In this book, I have used store-bought varieties for convenience. Be careful to simmer very gently once added to your soup.

Sumac

Native to the Middle East, sumac is a vibrant, coarse powder that has a lovely tangy, citrus flavor. You will find it in most supermarkets.

Tofu

Made from fresh soy milk that is curdled and then pressed into solid blocks. It is a fantastic source of protein, iron, and calcium. Although it has a very delicate flavor, it acts like a sponge for the flavors it is teamed with. You will find it in supermarkets, although Asian stores often stock superior varieties and brands.

Toasted sesame oil

I use toasted rather than plain sesame oil because it has a much more intense flavor. If it is not for you, feel free to use the plain variety.

Hominy

Hominy is dried corn and is a very popular ingredient used throughout Mexican cooking. You can buy it canned and ready to use or dried. Dried hominy requires the same treatment as dried beans—overnight soaking and boiling for 2 to 3 hours.

Tomatillos

Tomatillos are a staple of Mexican cuisine, similar in appearance to a green tomato but with papery skins. They are sweet and sour with a crunchy texture and can be ordered online when in season. Failing this, canned tomatillos will suffice. Green tomatoes are not a suitable substitute.

homemade stock

Homemade stock—a cooking process that many of us see as an unnecessary expenditure of our time. True, indeed, when time is of the essence. There are recipes where store-bought stock or bouillon cubes are perfectly adequate. As this is a soup book, and as every single one of the recipes in this book will be a million times better when made using homemade stock, I am pioneering the DIY version. It takes a little organization and planning to get through a stock recipe, but efforts are rewarded when one stock recipe gives you all you will need to create four soups each serving four people. That's a lot of soup and a lot of meals! Stock, and the majority of soups, freeze perfectly, so in the grand scheme of things you are spending time to save time. Plus, you are creating a meal that is infinitely more flavorful, healthy, and satisfying. Convinced yet?

To make things a little easier, I have simplified the lists of ingredients. Rather than give you three separate recipes, with three separate list of ingredients, I have created one generic stock recipe that changes only depending on the bones you are using. Cooking times vary somewhat, but each process is the same. I find this easier, as it helps to learn the recipes by heart, which inevitably helps it become second nature.

As always, there are two sides to every coin, and store-bought stock and bouillon cubes have been created for a very good reason. Time is something we often don't have to spare. There are really good bouillon cubes available, and many supermarkets now sell their own homemade stock. It is worth spending a little extra, if necessary, to buy quality. My favorite brands for bouillon cubes are Kallo (available online)—I find them the most naturally flavored and I always keep a stash of them in my pantry—and Knorr, which is also a good option. One thing I do find misleading at times is the guideline for cube to water ratio; I've had a few unpleasantly salty soups. Start off by using half a bouillon cube for the full amount of water recommended on the package and add the rest if you feel you need it.

Don't feel guilty if making stock is beyond your capabilities for whatever reason. However, I urge you to be open to it and perhaps try it at least once. If by purchasing this book you are setting off on a journey to cut back calories, or introduce more nutrition into your diet, any journey embarked on passionately from the very beginning stands a great chance of being successful!

Vegetable, Chicken, and Beef Stock

After making a couple of stocks, you will find you no longer need to consult the recipe. Furthermore, the list of ingredients is by no means set in stone; use whatever you have in the fridge. However, avoid vegetables such as broccoli, cabbage, cauliflower, turnips, beets, and potatoes.

Makes approx. 12 cups

2 onions, peeled and
  coarsely sliced

2 leeks

2 carrots

3 ribs of celery

6 sprigs of thyme

3 bay leaves

5 sprigs of parsley

10 black peppercorns

2¼ pounds raw chicken carcass
  (about 3) or 4½ pounds beef
  bones, if making chicken or
  beef stock

For vegetable stock, simply cover the vegetables with 16 cups of water, bring to a boil, reduce to a simmer and cook for 40 minutes. Allow to cool for 1 hour before ladling soup through a strainer lined with muslin or cheesecloth. Return to the heat, bring back to a boil, and reduce until you have about 12 cups.

For chicken or beef stock, rinse the bones under cold water and use scissors to remove any pieces of excess skin or fat.

Place the bones in a large stockpot and cover with 16 cups of water. Gently bring to a boil, skimming any foam that rises to the surface (bringing the stock to a boil before adding the vegetables makes this easier. Don't be tempted to add everything all at once). Reduce to a simmer, add all of the vegetables, and cook for 1½ to 2 hours for chicken and 4 to 5 hours for beef stock.

Let the stock cool for at least 30 minutes to allow the flavors to infuse. To strain, ladle it through a strainer lined with muslin or cheesecloth into a large bowl. Add a handful of ice cubes—this will encourage any fat to rise to the surface—and skim.

If any of the stocks are more than 12 cups, return to the heat and reduce. The stock will keep in the fridge for up to 1 week. Alternatively, freeze in 3-cup portions or make cubes (see page 16).

A More Intensely Flavored Stock

Roasting bones prior to cooking them in a stock creates a deeper, fuller flavor, and is the method I prefer. Simply place the bones into a roasting pan and roast at 400°F for 45 to 50 minutes. When ready, drain the fat and use some highly absorbent paper towels to pat off any fat still clinging to the bones. The bones are now ready to add to the stock.

Mushroom Stock

I love that this stock has only four ingredients that all come together to give you something really powerful. Of all the stocks, it is the punchiest in flavor and the most economical too. It will replace beef stock in many of the recipes in this book, making them suitable for vegans and vegetarians. Feel free to experiment with different types of mushrooms. Dried wild mushrooms will create an even richer flavor, and you could have these on standby in your pantry. This stock makes a smaller quantity than the other stocks in the book as I think it is better fresher. The recipe will give you enough stock for two soups serving four people.

Makes approx. 6 to 7 cups
1¾ pounds crimini mushrooms, quartered
1 small onion, quartered
2 carrots, coarsely chopped
2 garlic cloves, peeled

Place all of the ingredients into a stockpot with 8 cups of water. Bring to a boil, reduce to a simmer, and cook for 1 hour. Strain immediately. The stock will keep in the fridge for up to 3 days and freezes well.

Homemade Stock Cubes

This idea came about while chatting to my mother about my continual issue with space in my freezer. She had the brilliant idea to create frozen ice cubes of stock, rather than freezing it in batches. By reducing stock, you are condensing and concentrating its flavor dramatically, and reducing it enough to fit into an ice cube tray will give you premade stock cubes any time you need them. A little bit of time is required for this process, but I think it is worth it.

Makes approx. ½ cup
1 batch vegetable, chicken, beef, or mushroom stock

When you have made and strained a batch of stock, return to the stockpot and boil vigorously until reduced to approximately ½ cup. The beef and chicken stock will thicken and become a deep brown color, resembling caramel in both look and consistency. Keep a close eye on it when it is almost reduced, at this stage the process speeds up significantly and the reduced stock can easily evaporate too quickly and burn. Cool and pour into four cubes of an ice cube tray and freeze. To use, simply add one stock cube to 3 to 4 cups of water.

Japanese Dashi

Dashi is a Japanese stock that is known for its distinct umami flavor and it is used throughout Japanese cooking. Although the ingredients will most likely require some online shopping or a trip to your local Asian supermarket, this stock is easier to prepare and less expensive than many other stocks. It is as simple and straightforward as making a cup of tea. Making sure not to allow the stock to boil vigorously is about all the concentration this recipe requires. It forms the base for a traditional miso soup (see page 64) and creates a deliciously distinct and unique parsnip soup on page 44. It is made from kombu, a dried seaweed product, and bonito flakes or Katsoubushi, which comes from dried and smoked skipjack tuna. To make this stock vegan and vegetarian, simply omit the bonito flakes and add some dried shiitake mushrooms. You can make a second batch of stock by reboiling the ingredients. It will be slightly cloudier and have a stronger flavor, but it is still perfect for the purpose of the soups in this book.

Makes 4 cups

15-inch length of kombu, (approx. ½ ounce)

1 ounce (about 2¼ cups) shaved bonito flakes

Place the kombu with 4 cups of water in a saucepan over very low heat. Once the liquid has just begun to simmer, after about 20 to 25 minutes, remove from the heat immediately and add the bonito flakes. Allow the broth to sit for a couple of minutes before straining it through a strainer lined with muslin or cheesecloth. Cool and refrigerate for 3 to 4 days or freeze until needed.

A second stock of dashi can be made with the same ingredients. Simply add 4 cups of water to the same kombu and bonito flakes and barely simmer for 15 to 20 minutes. Add ¾ cup fresh bonito flakes to the stock and let stand for a couple of minutes before straining, as you have done above.

Turmeric and Lemongrass Paste

Making powerfully flavored pastes makes it very easy to create a wonderful broth without the time it takes to make stock. This paste is inspired by the flavors I experienced while traveling around Cambodia and Vietnam. A small hand-held blender will do all the work for you when creating this paste—it couldn't be easier!

Makes approx. 1 cup
(calories per tablespoon)

   calories 16 DF GF

Carbs 0.8g   Sugar 0.5g   Protein 0.4g   Fiber 0.5g   Fat 1.1g   Sat Fat 0.9g   Salt trace

2 fresh red bird's eye chiles
4 cloves of garlic, peeled
4 stalks of lemongrass, coarsely chopped
⅓ cup ginger, coarsely sliced
4 pink Asian shallots or 2 standard shallots
2½ teaspoons turmeric powder
⅔ cup fresh coconut (can be found
   prepared in supermarkets)
1 teaspoon shrimp paste

Blend all of the ingredients, with 4 to 5 tablespoons of water, to a paste using a mini hand-held blender. It will be reluctant to break down at first, but blend for a couple of minutes and you will get there!

Walnut Miso Paste

I first came across this in a little noodle bar called Koya in Soho, London. I was blown away by its addictive mellow flavor and wanted to recreate something similar here. It transforms the parsnip soup on page 44, and it adds a fantastic depth of flavor to the lunch noodle pots on pages 81–84. Store in your fridge and use to dress steamed vegetables or as a base for a salad dressing.

Makes approx. ⅓ cup
(calories per tablespoon)

    calories 15 DF V VE

Carbs 1.3g   Sugar 0.4g   Protein 0.5g   Fiber 0g   Fat 0.8g   Sat Fat 0.1g   Salt 0.3g

3 tablespoons walnuts, coarsely chopped
   (somewhere between chunky and fine)
2 tablespoons sweet white miso
1 tablespoon barley miso
1 tablespoon mirin
1 tablespoon tamari or light soy sauce

Toast the walnuts in a dry frying pan over medium heat until golden brown. Chopping them first is important to increase the surface area you are toasting—this flavor is an integral part of the paste. Mix the misos with the mirin and tamari or soy sauce. Add the toasted walnuts and mix thoroughly.

smooth soups

A smooth soup—a variety of ingredients cooked in stock and blended until silky smooth—is based on the simplest of concepts. However, this simplicity opens up a whole world of possibilities. There are infinite combinations you can play with by mixing and matching all kinds of vegetables and, at times, fruits, for a quirky layer of flavor. Spices, herbs, and garnishes can all serve to transform a simple idea into a remarkable dish.

I love to play with flavors, and a smooth soup is one of the most interesting ways to do this. There is a purity about a blended soup—a spoonful uninterrupted by texture that allows you to really appreciate and savor the qualities and characteristics of your chosen ingredients.

There are many classic combinations out there, all very well documented, so I have taken the soups in this chapter down a somewhat unexpected route. You will find that burning something is not always such a bad thing with the Blackened Tomato and Ancho Chile Soup, and that using a garnish of chilled zingy grapes cuts through the richness of a Thyme and Mustard Roasted Jerusalem Artichoke Soup. The sweet potato soup is anything but predictable flavored with sumac and pomegranate and piled high with crunchy nuts, cilantro, and pomegranate seeds.

These soups are very much a product of my imagination, and their difference makes them all the more delicious. They are fun and designed to get you excited about what you could be eating today!

blackened tomato and ancho chile with citrus sour cream

This recipe transforms a few humble tomatoes into a charred, smoky, sweet, rich, and deeply satisfying soup with a subtle hint of warmth from dried chiles. You will be asked to go against one of your main instincts in the kitchen and deliberately burn something. Crazy, I know—but it works!

Serves 4   calories 85   GF   V (DF and VE if not using sour cream)

Carbs 12.5g   Sugar 12.5g   Protein 2.5g   Fiber 4g   Fat 2g   Sat Fat 1g   Salt trace

3¾ pounds medium tomatoes
   on the vine
2 to 3 dried Ancho chiles
zest and juice of 1 lime
2 tablespoons sour cream
salt and pepper

Preheat the broiler to its highest temperature. Slice each tomato in half and arrange cut side up on a baking sheet. Place the pan on a rack as close to the broiler as possible and cook for 30 to 40 minutes until nicely blackened.

Meanwhile, place the dried chiles in a bowl with the tomato vines and cover with 2 cups boiling water. Set aside. Mix the lime zest with the sour cream and season with salt and pepper. Refrigerate until needed.

When the tomatoes are ready, carefully turn them over and broil for another 5 minutes, or until the skins are crisp and charred. This may happen quickly so keep a watchful eye.

When ready, discard the vines and transfer the tomatoes and all of their juices into a blender along with the chiles, their soaking water, and lime juice. Blend until smooth, season to taste, reheat, and serve garnished with a spoonful of citrus sour cream.

Tip: Store leftover dried chiles in an airtight jar. They will keep indefinitely.

golden beets, fennel, and saffron with poached rainbow trout

This is a meal in a bowl—extremely substantial and filling. You can play around with the fish you use. Some grilled scallops would be delicious with a little flourish of finely chopped chorizo. If you have any left over, try serving the fish cold on top of the reheated soup. The contrast of hot and cold works beautifully.

Serves 4 calories 137 DF GF

Carbs 9g   Sugar 8g   Protein 13g   Fiber 5g   Fat 4.5g   Sat Fat 0.8g   Salt 0.3g

3½ cups vegetable stock
1 to 2 fillets of rainbow trout
   (approx. 7 ounces), skin left on
½ tablespoon olive oil
1 small leek, sliced
1 garlic clove, chopped
2 sprigs of thyme, leaves picked
1 large fennel bulb, approximately
   9 to 10½ ounces, coarsely
   chopped (set aside tips for
   garnish)
14 ounces golden beets, peeled
   and grated
generous pinch of saffron
salt and pepper
dill, to garnish
1 lemon, cut into wedges, to serve

Bring the stock to a boil in a saucepan or frying pan deep enough to fit the fish. When simmering, place the fish in the liquid and cook gently for 5 minutes. When ready, transfer the fish to a plate or dish. Cover with foil and a kitchen towel to keep warm. Skim any froth, oils, or fat that have risen to the surface of the stock.

Meanwhile, heat the oil with 1 tablespoon of water in a medium saucepan and sauté the leek, garlic, and thyme for 5 minutes. Add the fennel, beets, saffron, and reserved stock and bring to a boil. Reduce to a simmer and cook for 20 minutes.

Blend until smooth, then return to the saucepan and keep over very low heat. Use a sharp-pointed knife to peel the skin from the fish and gently flake the flesh, being careful to leave behind any bones.

Pour the soup into heated bowls and top with the warm flaked rainbow trout. Season with salt and pepper, garnish with dill and the fennel tips, and serve immediately with a wedge of lemon.

miso-roasted butternut squash

This soup boasts an amazing depth of flavor thanks to the addition of some beautifully intense barley miso paste. You can play around with other types of miso here too. The nutritious properties of the paste deplete when cooked, so some is kept back and added when blending.

Serves 4   (GF if using GF miso)

Carbs 20g   Sugar 9g   Protein 4g   Fiber 4.8g   Fat 3.5g   Sat Fat 2.5g   Salt 0.9g

1 large butternut squash
   (approx. 2¼ pounds)
2½ tablespoons barley miso
1 tablespoon coconut oil, melted
   if solid
3 slices of ginger plus
   1½ tablespoons peeled
   and finely grated
2 garlic cloves, peeled
1 red chile
salt and pepper
1 lime, cut into four wedges,
   to serve
Crispy Sesame Tofu Fingers
   (page 28), to serve

Preheat the oven to 350°F.

Peel and halve the butternut squash, discarding the seeds, and coarsely chop into ¾-inch cubes. Place in a deep roasting pan. In a small bowl, mix together 1 tablespoon of barley miso with the melted coconut oil. Pour all over the squash, mixing well. Roast for 35 to 40 minutes, turning halfway through to ensure an even roast.

Meanwhile, prepare the stock: Place the slices of ginger, the garlic, and red chile in a saucepan with 3½ cups water. Bring to a boil and simmer with the lid on for 15 minutes. Remove from the heat and allow the flavors to infuse.

When the squash is ready, remove the aromatics from the stock and transfer to a blender with the roasted squash, remaining miso paste, and grated ginger. Blend until very smooth and season to taste with salt and pepper.

Serve with the lime wedges and crispy sesame tofu fingers.

crispy sesame tofu fingers

These are great served with the Miso-Roasted Butternut Squash soup on page 26. They also make an excellent snack, served with some chili sauce, such as Sriracha, or can be used as a garnish or crispy addition to a salad. Simply make them as cubes rather than long fingers.

Serves 4

Carbs 2.6g   Sugar 0.2g   Protein 6g   Fiber 0.1g   Fat 3.7g   Sat Fat 0.6g   Salt 0.4g

7 ounces firm tofu
2 tablespoons tamari or soy sauce
1 tablespoon ginger, finely grated
1½ tablespoons panko bread crumbs
½ tablespoon black sesame seeds
¼ teaspoon chile powder
generous pinch of salt and pepper
1 large free-range egg white, lightly whisked

Drain the tofu and pat dry with some paper towels. Squeeze as much liquid from the tofu as possible without breaking it up. Slice into four fingers and marinate in the tamari or soy sauce and ginger for a minimum of 30 minutes or overnight if possible.

Preheat the oven to 475°F. Remove the tofu from the marinade and brush off any clumps of ginger. Place between two pieces of paper towel and apply some gentle pressure to squeeze out any excess liquid.

Combine the bread crumbs, black sesame seeds, chile powder, and salt and pepper. Dip the tofu pieces into the egg white and then into the bread crumb mixture, making sure they are evenly coated.

Place on a baking sheet lined with parchment paper and bake for 5 minutes, turning halfway through, until nicely browned and crispy. Serve immediately alongside Miso-roasted Butternut Squash Soup (page 26).

thyme and mustard-roasted Jerusalem artichoke and garlic with red grapes

These knobbly vegetables are diamonds in the rough. They are next to impossible to peel, so I simply don't bother. There's a lot of flavor and goodness in the skin, so why waste time discarding it? Garlic becomes a sweeter, creamier, more subdued version of itself when roasted, so don't be alarmed by the quantity used here. And chilled red grapes provide some sharp sweetness, which cuts through the caramel tones of the roasted vegetables beautifully.

Serves 4   calories 172

Carbs 27g   Sugar 6.5g   Protein 5g   Fiber 11g   Fat 2.5g   Sat Fat 0.3g   Salt 0.8g

2 pounds Jerusalem artichokes, thoroughly washed and halved
½ head of garlic
5 to 6 sprigs of thyme, leaves picked, plus extra to serve
½ tablespoon olive oil
¾ tablespoon English or Dijon mustard
juice of ½ lemon
3 cups vegetable or chicken stock
small handful of chilled red grapes, quartered
salt and pepper

Preheat the oven to 350°F. Place the prepared artichokes on a baking sheet with the garlic and sprinkle the thyme all over.

Mix the olive oil, mustard, and lemon juice in a small bowl and drizzle all over the vegetables. Using your hands, make sure they are thoroughly coated. Season generously with salt and pepper and roast. The cooking time will vary slightly depending on what size Jerusalem artichokes you are using. Give them at least 30 minutes. If they are still firm after this time, cook until soft.

Bring the chicken stock to a boil. Now transfer, with the roasted vegetables, to a blender and process until very smooth. Serve topped with the chilled red grapes and fresh thyme leaves.

chilled cucumber, almond, and lemon

This soup is light, refreshing, zingy, rehydrating, and, most importantly, wonderfully cooling. You could chill the soup using plain ice cubes, but some decorative pomegranate ice cubes will add to the overall beauty of the dish, while adding some texture too.

Serves 4

Carbs 4.3g   Sugar 4.2g   Protein 1.4g   Fiber 1.1g   Fat 1g   Sat Fat 0.1g   Salt 0.1g

4 cups cucumber (about 1½ large cucumbers), coarsely chopped
1¼ cups unsweetened fresh almond milk (not UHT)
zest and juice of 1 lemon
2 to 3 sprigs of basil, leaves picked (about 10 leaves)
2 to 3 sprigs of mint, leaves picked (about 10 leaves)
a handful of pomegranate seeds (optional)
finely sliced cucumber (optional)

Blend all ingredients together until very smooth. Chill for up to two hours or overnight if possible. Serve in glasses.

To make the ice cubes, simply place some pomegranate seeds along with some finely sliced cucumber into an ice cube tray, cover with water, and freeze. I use small seedless cucumbers here, but you can use whatever is available.

Note: some edible flowers also look beautiful when frozen in ice cube trays.

pumpkin seed and prune rye soda bread

Soda bread is the Holy Grail of bread making—no kneading or rising required. Dry ingredients are gently mixed with wet before being baked, it couldn't be more straightforward! Rich and full of goodness, this loaf should be thinly sliced. It's a good idea to freeze some slices to have on hand when you need them. You can also use it to make croutons, crackers, and savory bread crumbs to serve as a garnish or side for lots of the soups in this book.

Makes 35 slices   calories 48   V

Carbs 6.3g   Sugar 1.1g   Protein 1.5g   Fiber 1.3g   Fat 1.5g   Sat Fat 0.2g   Salt 0.2g

¾ cup soft pitted prunes (about 6 small prunes)
1¾ cups stoneground rye flour
⅓ cup bread flour
1 teaspoon baking soda
1 teaspoon sea salt
1½ cups pumpkin seeds
¾ cup buttermilk
1 tablespoon oats

1-pound loaf pan, greased and lined

Preheat the oven to 350°F. Soak the prunes in ⅓ cup of boiling hot water.

Place the flours, baking soda, sea salt, and 1¼ cups of the pumpkin seeds in a medium bowl and mix well. Add the buttermilk to the prunes and soaking liquid and blend to a smooth puree. Pour into the dry ingredients, mixing very gently until you have a wet and sticky dough. Don't overmix, as this will result in a tough bread.

Transfer the dough to the prepared loaf pan, sprinkle with the remaining pumpkin seeds and the oats, and flatten down slightly. Bake for 40 minutes, turning upside down in the pan for the last 10 minutes of baking to get a nice even crust. Transfer to a wire rack to cool.

ideas for leftover soda bread

Soda bread crackers

These are so easy to make and provide a bit of crunch and texture when eaten alongside soup. It is important to slice the bread as thinly as possible, so best to make when the loaf is a few days old. Delicious topped with avocado and tomato, a little scrambled egg, or a finely chopped salsa of tomato, scallion, cucumber, avocado, and corn. Use with recipes such as the Aromatic Dhal soup (page 122).

Serves 4

Carbs 11g   Sugar 0.4g   Protein 1.6g   Fiber 0.5g   Fat 0.3g   Sat Fat 0.1g   Salt 0.1g

8 very thin slices of soda bread (to serve 4)

Preheat the oven to 400°F. Lay the slices on a baking sheet and cook for 8 to 10 minutes, turning halfway through and keeping a close eye to ensure they are not burning. You can make a batch of these and store in an airtight container. They will keep for about a week.

Croutons

Croutons are a great garnish for soups, and this soda bread version is delicious. For extra flavor, rub each slice with a clove of garlic before cutting.

Serves 4

Carbs 7g   Sugar 1.2g   Protein 1.8g   Fiber 1.3g   Fat 1.6g   Sat Fat 0.3g   Salt trace

3 slices soda bread, each cut into 8
½ tablespoon canola or olive oil
salt and pepper

Preheat the oven to 350°F. Dress the croutons with the oil, salt, and pepper and transfer to a baking sheet. Bake for 10 to 12 minutes, checking and turning a couple of times while cooking. They will keep for 2 to 3 days in an airtight container.

Savory Bread Crumbs

This is a great way to add texture, substance, and another layer of flavor to lots of soups. The bread crumbs cook extremely quickly so keep a close eye on them. Once cooked, I like to add herbs such as thyme, tarragon, oregano, or rosemary. Chile powder is nice too, as is ground ginger or smoked paprika. A half teaspoon of miso stirred through the bread crumbs before cooking is also delicious.

Serves 4

Carbs 8g   Sugar 0.3g   Protein 1.2g   Fiber 0.4g   Fat 0.2g   Sat Fat 0.1g   Salt 0.1g

3 slices bread, processed into
   bread crumbs
salt and pepper

Preheat the oven to 400°F. Process three slices of bread into bread crumbs, spread in a thin layer on a baking sheet, and season with salt and pepper. Cook for no more than 3 minutes, checking a few times to prevent burning. The bread crumbs will continue to crisp as they cool. They will keep for 2 to 3 days in an airtight container.

sichuan-roasted red bell pepper with five-spice edamame relish

Sichuan peppercorns are native to the Sichuan province of China, but are actually the dried berries of a type of ash tree and have a lemony and peppery fragrance. Beautifully aromatic, they leave an amazing numbing or tingling sensation on the palate, giving this soup a cooling rather than warming effect.

Serves 4 calories 125   (GF if using tamari)

Carbs 16g   Sugar 16g   Protein 5.5g   Fiber 8g   Fat 2g   Sat Fat 0.3g   Salt 2g

1 tablespoon Sichuan peppercorns
2 garlic cloves, peeled
pinch of salt
3 tablespoons tamari or dark soy sauce
2¼ pounds red bell peppers, each seeded and cut into 8 (set aside ½ a pepper for Five-spice Edamame Relish, below)
2 medium tomatoes, quartered
1 medium red onion, peeled and coarsely sliced
2¾ cups vegetable or chicken stock

For the Five-spice Edamame Relish (30 calories per serving; not suitable for freezing)
½ cup frozen edamame
½ red bell pepper (see above), diced
⅛ teaspoon five-spice powder
juice of ½ a lime
pinch of salt

Preheat the oven to 400°F. Toast the peppercorns in a dry frying pan for 2 minutes. Grind in a mortar and pestle, along with the garlic and salt, to a coarse paste. Add the tamari or soy sauce and mix well.

Place the peppers and tomatoes in a large bowl with the sliced onion and pour over the Sichuan peppercorn mixture. Use your hands to thoroughly mix, ensuring all the vegetables are coated. Divide between two baking sheets and roast for 40 minutes, turning occasionally. When ready, transfer to a large bowl, cover with plastic wrap, and let stand for 10 minutes.

For the relish, simmer the edamame for 5 minutes, refresh under cold water, and pat dry. Mix with the red bell pepper, five-spice powder, lime juice, and salt. Refrigerate until needed.

Heat the stock and, when almost boiling, pour three quarters of it into a blender and add the vegetables. Blend until silky smooth and add enough stock to achieve your desired consistency. Return to the saucepan and bring back to a boil before serving with the edamame relish.

Note: if using an immersion blender for this soup, you may need to pass it through a strainer for a smooth consistency.

corn, lemongrass, and turmeric

This is remarkably decadent considering nothing creamy is added, which would often be the case with a corn-based soup. A fantastic filling lunch, or serve in small portions as an appetizer to a more formal meal.

Serves 4 calories 114 DF GF

Carbs 11.5g   Sugar 3.5g   Protein 5g   Fiber 3.7g   Fat 4.5g   Sat Fat 2g   Salt trace

1 medium leek, trimmed, halved, and coarsely chopped
¾ tablespoon coconut oil, melted if solid
3 tablespoons Turmeric and Lemongrass Paste (page 18)
3½ cups corn, freshly removed from 4 to 5 cobs
salt and pepper
fresh cilantro, to garnish

Sauté the leek in ½ tablespoon coconut oil and 1 tablespoon water until softened, about 5 to 7 minutes, stirring occasionally. Stir in the paste and cook for a couple of minutes. Add all but ¾ cup of the corn along with 3¾ cups water and the cobs for added flavor. Bring to a boil, reduce to a simmer, and cook for 15 minutes.

Heat the broiler to high. Place the reserved corn along with the remaining ¼ tablespoon of coconut oil onto a baking sheet, mix together, and place under the broiler for 5 to 8 minutes. When starting to char, remove, season, and set aside.

When the soup is ready, let cool a little before removing the cobs, then blend until smooth. Pour through a strainer to achieve a silky smooth soup, season to taste, and serve garnished with the charred corn and some fresh cilantro.

celeriac with horseradish, lemon, and parsley

This combination of flavors is one of my all-time favorites and I never enjoy it more than when it is presented in a lusciously smooth bowl of soup. Enjoy with a few slices of Pumpkin Seed and Prune Soda Bread (page 32).

Serves 4

calories 144   GF   V

Carbs 17g   Sugar 7g   Protein 6g   Fiber 10g   Fat 3.5g   Sat Fat 1g   Salt 0.5g

1 small leek, trimmed, cleaned, and coarsely sliced
1 garlic clove, coarsely chopped
1 medium potato, peeled and diced
½ tablespoon olive oil
1 small celeriac (about 1¼ pounds), peeled and coarsely chopped into ½-inch cubes
2 peeled strips of lemon rind
3 cups vegetable stock
⅓ cup parsley, stalks reserved and leaves coarsely chopped
1 bay leaf
2 tablespoons freshly grated horseradish (use from a jar if you can't find fresh)
1 teaspoon Dijon mustard
1 cup 1% milk
salt and pepper
juice of 1 lemon, to serve

In a saucepan, sauté the leek, garlic, and potato in the olive oil and 1 tablespoon of water over medium heat for 5 minutes, stirring frequently. Add a splash more water if the vegetables stick to the pan.

Add the celeriac, lemon rind, and stock. Tie the reserved parsley stalks and bay leaf together with a piece of string and add to the soup. Bring to a gentle simmer and cook with the lid on for 30 minutes.

Five minutes before the soup is finished, remove the herbs and lemon rind. Stir in the grated horseradish, mustard, and milk. Simmer for the remaining 5 minutes, and then blend, adding a splash of water or stock if the soup is too thick for you. Season with salt and pepper. Stir the lemon juice and chopped parsley through the soup immediately before serving.

sweet potato, sumac, and pomegranate with roasted peanuts, cilantro, and lime

Sometimes I find sweet potato soup a little too sweet, but not here—teamed with citrusy sumac, sour pomegranate, aromatic cilantro, and crunchy roasted peanuts, it is what a bowl of fun should look like!

Serves 4   (V/VE if using vegetable stock)

Carbs 32g   Sugar 16g   Protein 5g   Fiber 6g   Fat 6g   Sat Fat 2g   Salt 0.2g

1 medium onion, coarsely chopped

2 garlic cloves, coarsely chopped

1 red chile, seeded and coarsely chopped

1 teaspoon sumac

½ tablespoon coconut oil

3 cups sweet potatoes, peeled and chopped into ¾-inch cubes

3 to 4 vine tomatoes, coarsely chopped (about 1¾ cups)

3½ cups chicken or vegetable stock

1½ tablespoons pomegranate molasses

Garnish

small bunch of cilantro leaves

½ cup roasted salted peanuts, coarsely chopped

seeds from ½ pomegranate

a few pinches of sumac

1 lime, cut into four wedges

Sauté the onion, garlic, chile, and sumac in the coconut oil and 1 tablespoon of water until soft and translucent—about 5 minutes.

Add the sweet potatoes, tomatoes, and stock, bring to a boil, and then simmer with the lid on for about 20 minutes, until the potatoes are tender. Let cool a little before adding the pomegranate molasses. Blend until silky smooth and season.

Garnish with the cilantro, chopped peanuts, pomegranate seeds, sumac, and wedge of lime.

Tip: if you have a gluten intolerance and wish to use store-bought peanuts, make sure they are gluten-free.

parsnip and walnut miso soup

Parsnips and the Walnut Miso Paste make a beautiful pairing. Homemade dashi is what really makes this soup unique and is worth the little extra effort to achieve the resulting flavor. Served with Sriracha Parsnip Chips (opposite) this soup makes for a sweet, spicy bowl of joy.

Serves 4   calories 165   DF

Carbs 23g   Sugar 10g   Protein 4g   Fiber 7.5g   Fat 5g   Sat Fat 0.6g   Salt 1g

I garlic clove, finely chopped

I to 2 large shallots, chopped

1½ tablespoons ginger, coarsely chopped

½ tablespoon toasted sesame oil

1¼ pounds parsnips, peeled and cut into ¾-inch cubes

3 cups Japanese Dashi, (page 17)

2½ tablespoons Walnut Miso Paste (page 18)

Sauté the garlic, shallot, and ginger in the toasted sesame oil and I tablespoon of water for about 5 minutes until soft and translucent. Add the parsnips and dashi, bring to a boil, and simmer gently with the lid on for 25 to 30 minutes, until the parsnips are tender.

Transfer to a blender and process until silky smooth. Stir in the Walnut Miso Paste; alternatively, swirl a spoonful of the paste into the soup before serving. Garnish with Sriracha Parsnip Chips.

vegetable chips

Vegetable chips couldn't be easier to make and are a delicious garnish for many soups, and make a great healthy snack. They are best eaten the day they are cooked; they won't keep in an airtight container.
A mandolin will make your life so much easier here.

Sriracha Parsnip Chips

Serves 4 as a garnish
(calories per chip)

Carbs 0.5g   Sugar 0.2g   Protein 0.1g   Fiber 0.2g   Fat 0.0g   Sat Fat 0.0g   Salt trace

1 large parsnip, washed and peeled
1 tablespoon Sriracha
salt and pepper

Preheat the oven to 300°F. Thinly slice the parsnip into circles, about ⅛-inch thick, or use a potato peeler to create long, thin strips. Coat with the Sriracha, salt, and pepper and lay flat on a baking sheet lined with parchment paper. These crisps can take minutes to cook, depending on the size of the parsnips. Give them 5 minutes, and check regularly, removing any that are cooking quicker. Bigger ones may require a minute or so longer.

Beet Chips

Serves 4 as a garnish
(calories per chip)

Carbs 0.1g   Sugar 0.1g   Protein trace   Fiber trace   Fat 0.2g   Sat Fat 0.0g   Salt trace

1 beet, washed and peeled
   (or try a mix of red, pink, and golden)
1 tablespoon canola or olive oil
flavor ideas: ground fennel seeds, sumac, and fresh thyme
salt and pepper

Preheat the oven to 300°F. Thinly slice the beet into perfect circles about ⅛-inch thick. Thoroughly coat with the oil, salt, and pepper and any other flavor you have chosen. Lay on a baking sheet lined with parchment paper and bake for 15 minutes, turning halfway. You may need to do this in batches or use two baking sheets. Check every 5 minutes, and remove any that are already cooked—smaller chips will cook quicker. Let cool before serving.

Peppered Sweet Potato Chips

Serves 4 as a garnish
(calories per chip)

 calories 12   DF GF V VE

Carbs 1.7g   Sugar 0.5g   Protein 0.1g   Fiber 0.3g   Fat 0.5g   Sat Fat 0.0g   Salt 0.1g

½ sweet potato, washed
   and peeled
1 tablespoon canola oil
½ teaspoon freshly ground
   pepper (a mix of black, pink,
   and white peppercorns would
   be nice, too)
generous pinch of salt

Preheat the oven to 300°F. Thinly slice the sweet potato into circles. Alternatively, you could use a potato peeler to create long, thin strips. Coat with the oil, pepper, and salt and lay on a lined baking sheet. You may need to do this in batches, or use two baking sheets. Bake for 12 minutes, checking regularly and removing any that are cooking faster. Let cool before serving.

broths and consommés

My love affair with broths began when I was traveling in Southeast Asia. Every day for breakfast, lunch, or dinner we would have a bowl of hot broth brimming with silky noodles, fresh vegetables, and herbs. No two were ever the same and not one failed to blow me away. It sparked a profound passion and respect for the wonder that is a bowl of broth—a perfectly balanced blend of flavors, effortlessly healthy and wonderfully wholesome.

It can be as simple as a miso soup, adorned with nothing more than tofu, scallions, and wakame, or as complex as the Hoi An New Wives' Broth, which is a celebration of harmonious yet dynamic flavors. Some, such as Wonton Soup, are well-known favorites, whereas others, such as the Korean Steak Tartare in Broth, are my own adaptation of a traditional dish. An intensely flavored Turmeric and Lemongrass paste is a quick-fire way to add bold flavor to a broth without needing much time. The laborious aspect of a consommé is overcome by applying the same technique to fruits and vegetables, providing recipes that are a lot less time-consuming, but incredibly flavorful. The essence of tomatoes is captured in the Tomato Consommé Cooler, boasting flavor so invigorating, it will awaken each and every taste bud.

Broths are, at times, somewhat demanding of either time or effort. However, the satisfaction to be gained from stepping off the treadmill to spend a little uninterrupted time in the kitchen will make it all worthwhile. These are recipes worth shutting out the world for!

sea bream, coconut, and lime broth

While in Cambodia, I ate the most unusual crab and lime soup—like nothing I had ever tasted, its vibrancy and clarity snapped my senses awake. This recipe is a nod to that memory.

Serves 4    calories 216   DF   GF

· ·

Carbs 16.8g   Sugar 14.5g   Protein 25.3g   Fiber 3g   Fat 4.5g   Sat Fat 0.4g   Salt 2.8g

· ·

2¾ cups coconut water

3 stalks of lemongrass, bruised and cut into ¾-inch lengths

5 kaffir lime leaves

4 garlic cloves, peeled

8 Asian shallots, peeled and quartered

2 tablespoons ginger, peeled and sliced

2 tablespoons fish sauce

1 sea bream or sea bass (approx. 18 ounces to 1½ pounds), gutted and cleaned

4 red bird's eye chiles, 1 halved, others finely sliced

½ cup each of Thai basil, mint, and cilantro, leaves picked

3 scallions, thinly sliced

2 cups bean sprouts

juice of 3 limes

Mango relish

½ mango, peeled and shredded

1 red bird's eye chile, finely chopped

½ tablespoon fish sauce

½ teaspoon black pepper

Place all of the ingredients up to and including the sea bream and the halved bird's eye chile with 4 cups of water in a deep heavy-bottomed saucepan wide enough to hold the fish lying flat. Bring to a simmer and cook for 15 minutes.

Meanwhile, make the mango relish: Combine all ingredients, mix well, and taste for seasoning.

Divide the finely sliced bird's eye chiles between four bowls, along with the herbs, scallions, and bean sprouts.

When cooked, remove the fish from the broth, peel away the skin, and carefully remove the white flesh from the bones. Divide between the bowls.

Stir the lime juice through the broth, and taste for seasoning. If needed, add a dash of fish sauce. Strain and pour over the ingredients in each bowl. Garnish with the mango relish and serve immediately.

Note: kaffir lime leaves can be found online or in Asian supermarkets, often in the freezer section. If you can't find any fresh or frozen, many big supermarkets stock dried leaves.

Not suitable for freezing

green vegetable broth with pistou chicken skewers

This soup is a gorgeous contrast of crunchy refreshing vegetables and deliciously charred chicken skewers. Get them on the grill if you have one going!

Serves 2

calories 299 GF

Carbs 13g   Sugar 7g   Protein 37g   Fiber 5g   Fat 10g   Sat Fat 1.5g   Salt 0.3g

For the pistou
2 garlic cloves, peeled
1¼ cups basil, coarsely chopped
1 tablespoon olive oil
1 medium ripe tomato, coarsely
    chopped

For the skewers and broth
2 small chicken breasts
    (approx. 9 ounces)
⅓ cup buttermilk
wooden skewers, soaked
1 to 2 large shallots, finely diced
2 garlic cloves, finely chopped
3 sun-dried tomatoes, coarsely
    chopped
½ tablespoon olive oil
1 tablespoon tomato paste
4 cups vegetable stock
1¼ cups baby zucchini, sliced
½ cup asparagus, diced
½ cup green beans, trimmed and
    cut into ½-inch lengths
½ cup sugar snap peas,
    cut into 3 pieces

First make the pistou: Pound the garlic with a pinch of salt in a mortar and pestle until smooth. Add the basil and grind until almost smooth. Add the olive oil, then the tomato, and pound everything to a coarse paste (or use a mini hand-held blender for this). Season to taste.

Place the chicken breasts between two pieces of plastic wrap and, using a rolling pin, bash until they are nice and thin. When ready, slice each breast into four strips lengthwise. Mix half of the pistou with the buttermilk, add the chicken, and marinate for a minimum of 30 minutes, or overnight if possible. When ready, thread the chicken onto the soaked skewers and set aside.

In a medium saucepan, sauté the shallot, garlic, and sun-dried tomato in the oil and 1 tablespoon of water until softened. Add the tomato paste and stock, bring to a boil, and simmer for 10 minutes.

Meanwhile, place a grill pan over high heat and cook the chicken skewers for 3 to 4 minutes on each side.

Add the vegetables to the broth and simmer for 3 to 4 minutes. Season to taste. Serve with the skewers alongside, and the remaining pistou to stir through.

Broth only suitable for freezing

korean steak tartare (yukhoe) in broth

Yukhoe is a Korean steak tartare dish, traditionally served with Asian pear, egg yolk, and pine nuts. Here it sits within a punchy, spicy broth, with gochujang, a Korean chile paste. This is an intensely flavoured soup and epitomizes using the very best ingredients and treating them in quite a simple way.

Serves 4   (GF if using tamari)

Carbs 6g   Sugar 6g   Protein 12.5g   Fiber 1.1g   Fat 5g   Sat Fat 1.7g   Salt 2.8g

7 ounces high-quality filet mignon

1 garlic clove, peeled

2 tablespoons ginger, peeled and finely chopped or grated

3 tablespoons tamari or light soy sauce

1 teaspoon toasted sesame oil

1 teaspoon honey

3 teaspoons Korean chile powder (if using plain chile powder ½ teaspoon is sufficient)

1 scallion, finely chopped

3 cups Mushroom Stock (page 16)

2 teaspoons gochujang

2 teaspoons mirin (optional)

1½ tablespoons parsley, finely chopped

1½ teaspoons black or white sesame seeds, toasted

Slice the beef into very thin strips, then cut into tiny dice. It is very important to chop the beef as finely as possible. Pound the garlic and ginger in a mortar and pestle to a smooth paste and add two tablespoons of the tamari or soy sauce, the sesame oil, honey, and chile powder. (or chop the garlic and ginger together until they resemble a paste.) Thoroughly mix the resulting sauce with the beef, along with the scallion, and chill in the fridge until needed.

Gently heat the mushroom stock until just boiling, then reduce the heat to keep it at a simmer. Add the gochujang, remaining tamari or soy sauce, and mirin, if using, and whisk to dissolve the chile paste. Taste and adjust to your liking if necessary.

Just before serving, add half of the parsley to the tartare and mix well. Neatly divide the mixture between four bowls and pour in the broth. Top the tartare with the remaining parsley and the sesame seeds. Serve immediately.

Note: the broth base can be made ahead and frozen, but the tartare must be made fresh. Korean chile powder and gochujang can be found in Asian supermarkets.

wonton soup

You are most likely to find wonton wrappers online or in Asian supermarkets. Buy a few packets, and pop what you don't use in the freezer. Divide and freeze in batches based on the number called for in a particular recipe (I find 12 to 16 is a good quantity, or 8 in the case of the recipe for wonton crisps—see page 58).

Serves 4 calories 205 DF

Carbs 17g   Sugar 1.7g   Protein 18g   Fiber 1.6g   Fat 6g   Sat Fat 1.6g   Salt 1.5g

5½ ounces raw shrimp, deveined and finely chopped
5½ ounces ground pork
8 dried Chinese mushrooms, rehydrated and finely chopped
⅔ cup chives, finely chopped
I teaspoon oyster sauce
pinch of salt
1½ teaspoons sesame oil
2 teaspoons shaoxing wine
2 teaspoons tamari or light soy sauce
12 wonton wrappers
5 cups vegetable stock
generous pinch of white pepper
4 baby bok choy, quartered

In a bowl, mix together the shrimp, pork, mushrooms, chives, oyster sauce, and salt with I teaspoon each of the sesame oil, shaoxing wine, and tamari or soy sauce.

Working with one wonton wrapper at a time, keeping the rest covered with a damp kitchen towel so that they don't dry out, lay the wrapper in front of you, so that it is in the shape of a diamond. Place a tablespoon of the mixture in the middle and, using your finger, moisten the edges of the wrapper with a little water. Fold the wrapper in half so that it is the shape of a triangle and press the edges together to seal. Now bring the two bottom corners together, dampen the edges again, and seal. It should resemble tortellini.

Fill a large saucepan with water and bring to a gentle simmer. Cook the wontons in batches, for 5 minutes at a time, turning over halfway through cooking. It is important not to vigorously boil the water, otherwise the wontons will fall apart.

Meanwhile, in a separate pan, bring the stock to a boil and season with the remaining sesame oil, tamari or soy sauce, shaoxing rice wine, and white pepper. Add the bok choy and cook for a couple of minutes.

Divide the wontons between four bowls, along with the bok choy, then pour in the stock and serve immediately.

Tips: If you can't find dried Chinese mushrooms, use dried shiitake or porcini mushrooms, which can be found in most big supermarkets.

You can make the wontons ahead and freeze them uncooked. Simply place on some parchment paper in a plastic container, cover with a tight-fitting lid, and freeze. Cook them from frozen, adding 2 to 3 minutes to the cooking time.

hoisin sesame seed wonton crisps

Wonton wrappers can be kept in batches in the freezer ready to make these crisps at the drop of a hat. They are a quick and easy side to throw together for a soup and are a delicious snack all on their own. They will keep for a couple of days in an airtight container.

Serves 4 calories 81 (VE if using vegetarian hoisin sauce)

Carbs 9g   Sugar 0.7g   Protein 2.8g   Fiber 0.6g   Fat 3.5g   Sat Fat 0.6g   Salt 0.2g

8 wonton wrappers
1 tablespoon hoisin sauce
1½ tablespoons sesame seeds, white or black or a mixture
salt and pepper

Preheat the oven to 350°F and line a baking sheet with parchment paper. Brush both sides of each wonton wrapper with the hoisin sauce and place on the baking sheet. Scatter the sesame seeds all over, with a small pinch of salt and pepper. Bake for 8 to 10 minutes, keeping a close eye to ensure they don't burn. When golden brown and crisp, remove from the oven and transfer to a cooling rack. They will continue to crisp as they cool.

Not suitable for freezing

braised wild mushroom broth

Braising wild mushrooms gently coaxes out enough flavor without stripping them of their character—a simple but effective way to preserve their delicacy and beauty. If you can't get your hands on wild mushrooms, simply use a mixture of varieties such as button, crimini, and portobello. Soda bread croutons are tasty served with this soup for a little texture and extra substance.

Serves 4 calories 58 (V/VE if using vegetable stock)

Carbs 5g   Sugar 4g   Protein 4g   Fiber 3g   Fat 2g   Sat Fat 0.3g   Salt 0.1g

½ onion, finely diced
1 celery rib, finely diced
2 medium carrots, peeled and
   finely diced
1 garlic clove, finely chopped
½ tablespoon olive oil
1¼ pounds wild mushrooms,
   such as chanterelles, morels,
   or a mixture of different kinds
2 sprigs of rosemary, leaves
   picked and coarsely chopped
   (alternatively, use thyme)
4 cups beef or vegetable stock
1 sprig of tarragon (optional)
small bunch of parsley, coarsely
   chopped, to garnish
Soda Bread Croutons, to serve
   (page 34)

Preheat the oven to 400°F.

In an ovenproof casserole dish or saucepan, sauté the onion, celery, carrot, and garlic in the olive oil and 1 tablespoon of water for 10 minutes, stirring from time to time. Add a splash more water if the vegetables stick to the pan.

Meanwhile, carefully clean the mushrooms using a soft-bristled brush or some damp paper towels. Add to the saucepan with the rosemary and sauté, stirring, for about 5 minutes until nicely softened.

Add the stock and tarragon (if using) and bring to a boil. Cover with a lid and transfer to the oven for 20 to 25 minutes. When ready, remove the tarragon and serve garnished with some freshly chopped parsley and soda bread croutons.

Tip: To make this dairy- and gluten-free, simply leave out the soda bread croutons.

fladelsuppe (german crepe soup)

When I'm not feeling well, this is how I like to have my chicken broth—adorned with one of my ultimate comfort foods, crepes. It may sound like an unusual combination, but trust me, this is the perfect soup for when you feel poorly. Delicate but wholesome chicken broth soaked up with deliciously simple yet substantial crepes, it's perfect for boosting energy and making you feel a bit more human.

Serves 4 calories 185   (V if using vegetable stock)

Carbs 17g   Sugar 2g   Protein 7g   Fiber 0.8g   Fat 10g   Sat Fat 2.2g   Salt 0.2g

⅔ cup all-purpose flour
⅔ cup 1% milk
2 large free-range eggs, whisked
olive or canola oil for frying
5 cups chicken stock
generous pinch of nutmeg
small bunch of chives, finely
   chopped
salt and pepper

Place the flour in a medium bowl and gradually whisk in the milk and eggs until it's the consistency of half-and-half. Season generously with salt and pepper.

Heat a medium-sized skillet or frying pan and brush with a little oil. Pour in a ladle of the crepe mix, swirling so that it spreads and covers the pan. After 3 to 4 minutes and once the crepe has a little color, flip it over and cook on the other side. Repeat to make three more crepes.

Bring the chicken stock to a boil and season with salt, pepper, and nutmeg.

Roll up the crepes and slice into thin shreds. Divide between four bowls. Pour over the hot stock, garnish with chives, and serve.

pea and mushroom rare beef tenderloin broth

This is a real feel-good soup, celebrating the flavor, texture, and pure, unadulterated nutrition of barely cooked meat and vegetables. To make this soup vegetarian, simply replace the beef with some firm tofu.

Serves 4 calories 115 DF GF

Carbs 6.5g   Sugar 2.5g   Protein 12.3g   Fiber 2.7g   Fat 3.8g   Sat Fat 1.1g   Salt 1.3g

5 cups Mushroom Stock
(page 16)
2 tablespoons sweet white
miso paste
I tablespoon tamari or light
soy sauce
¾ cup edamame
I cup sugar snap peas, each
cut into three
4 small radishes, thinly sliced
I cup enoki mushrooms, roots
removed if still attached
4 baby bok choy (2 normal-sized
ones will also suffice), sliced
4½ ounces beef tenderloin,
sliced into thin strips

Bring the stock to a boil and then reduce to barely a simmer. Whisk in the miso and tamari or soy sauce and taste for seasoning.

Add all of the vegetables and simmer for no longer than 2 to 3 minutes. Divide between four bowls and top with the sliced beef. If you prefer more well-done meat, place the tenderloin slices in the bowl before pouring in the hot broth. This will cook the beef. Serve immediately.

Not suitable for freezing

miso soup with tofu and scallions

Although I normally choose to serve this soup in its simplest form, once you have the base figured out, you can add pretty much anything you like. For a soup that is so deeply satisfying and flavorful, this is about the easiest one to make. Experiment with different types of miso pastes to find your perfect flavor. You can find instant dashi in Asian supermarkets if making your own is a stretch too far.

Serves 4

Carbs 4.4g   Sugar 0.8g   Protein 7.3g   Fiber 1g   Fat 4.4g   Sat Fat 0.6g   Salt 1.3g

I tablespoon wakame seaweed

5 cups Japanese Dashi
   (page 17)

3½ tablespoons miso paste
   (I use 2½ tablespoons sweet
   white miso and I tablespoon
   barley miso)

I teaspoon rice vinegar

7 ounces silken tofu, drained
   and cubed

To garnish

4 scallions

black sesame seeds (optional)

I teaspoon toasted sesame oil
   (optional)

Soak the dried wakame in hot water for 10 minutes until soft, then cut into thin strips.

Gently heat the dashi in a medium saucepan, until just about simmering. Whisk a spoonful of hot dashi into the miso paste to loosen it, then add this to the rest of the stock, along with the vinegar. It is very important not to boil this soup, as the nutritional value of miso depletes when overheated. You want to keep it at just below boiling point at all times.

Add the tofu and wakame, divide between four bowls, and garnish with scallions and, if using, black sesame seeds and a few drops of sesame oil.

Not suitable for freezing

hoi an new wives' broth with shrimp dumplings

This is an adaptation of a recipe I learned to cook in Hoi An, Vietnam. It is traditionally served ceremonially, a new wife making it for her husband's family, and its success, or lack thereof, will signify her future success as a wife. A perfect example of how integral food is to the lives of the Vietnamese (pictured on page 66).

Serves 4

Carbs 12.5g   Sugar 12g   Protein 17g   Fiber 8g   Fat 2.5g   Sat Fat 0.4g   Salt 4g

For the stock
1 small savoy cabbage
2 teaspoons fish sauce
½ teaspoon palm sugar
  (or superfine sugar)
½ teaspoon salt

For the shrimp dumplings
4 scallions, coarsely chopped
10½ ounces fresh raw shrimp
1 garlic clove, finely chopped
2 tablespoons chives, finely
  chopped
½ cup cilantro, coarsely chopped
1 tablespoon fish sauce
½ teaspoon salt

For the soup base
½ tablespoon toasted sesame oil
2 scallions, finely chopped
1 shallot, finely chopped
⅓ cup shrimp dumpling mixture
1¼ cups crimini mushrooms,
  finely chopped

First make the stock: Remove the tough outer leaves of the cabbage, reserve two, wash, and cut in half. Place in a medium saucepan with 7 cups of water, fish sauce, palm sugar, and salt. Simmer for 20 minutes. When ready, strain and return to medium heat to keep warm.

Meanwhile, make the dumplings: Place the scallions into a mini food processor and pulse until finely chopped. Add the shrimp, garlic, chives, cilantro, fish sauce, and salt and pulse until just combined. You don't want a puree, so pulse with caution! Set aside ⅓ cup of the dumpling mix. Using wet hands, shape the rest into 16 little dumplings, weighing about ¾ ounce each. Chill in the fridge until needed. This can be done up to a day in advance.

To make the soup base, heat the sesame oil and 1 tablespoon water in a frying pan and cook the scallions and shallot for a couple of minutes before adding the reserved dumpling mixture and mushrooms. Mix well to ensure the shrimp mixture breaks down rather than cooking in chunks. Add the fish sauce, salt, and pepper and cook for another 5 minutes.

Prepare the remaining cabbage: Strip the leaves and shred as finely as possible. Bring the stock to a boil and

1 tablespoon fish sauce
½ teaspoon salt
½ teaspoon black pepper
2 carrots, peeled and finely
  sliced

Garnishes
cilantro
sliced scallions
sliced red chile

blanch the cabbage and sliced carrots for no more than
2 minutes. Refresh under cold water and set aside. Now
poach the dumplings: Place them in the gently simmering
stock for 5 minutes, turning them as they cook.

To finish, divide the cabbage, mushrooms, carrots,
and the shrimp mixture between four bowls, along with
the dumplings. Pour over the boiling stock, garnish with
cilantro, scallions, and sliced red chile, and serve.

Not suitable for freezing

umami broth with five-spice asparagus, pork, and chive dumplings

When in Vietnam, I had a soup made with ground pork fried with five-spice
powder and other aromatics, served in a deliciously flavored broth with
Chinese chives and tofu. I can still close my eyes and taste every mouthful
of that soup. The broth they used took twenty-four hours to make—this one
takes a lot less time, but packs a powerful punch and is the perfect vehicle
for the flavors I remember so distinctly.

Serves 4 calories 212

Carbs 22g   Sugar 2.2g   Protein 16.7g   Fiber 1.1g   Fat 6.1g   Sat Fat 1.7g   Salt 2.7g

For the broth
¼ cup sun-dried tomatoes
¼ cup porcini mushrooms
2 garlic cloves, peeled
approx. ¾ ounce Parmesan rind
4 black olives
1 bay leaf

Place all of the broth ingredients up to and including the
bay leaf in a large saucepan and cover with 6 cups
of water. Slowly bring to a boil, then simmer for about
35 to 40 minutes. Pass through a strainer lined with
muslin or cheesecloth. Return to a clean saucepan and
add the balsamic vinegar and fish sauce.

½ tablespoon balsamic vinegar

1½ tablespoons fish sauce

For the dumplings

6 ounces lean ground pork

3 asparagus spears, finely
chopped

3 tablespoons chives, finely
chopped

1¼ teaspoons five-spice powder

1 tablespoon tamari or dark soy
sauce

¾ tablespoon fish sauce

1 teaspoon hoisin sauce
(or a pinch of sugar)

generous pinch of black pepper

½ teaspoon cornstarch

16 gyoza wrappers (available from
Asian supermarkets, often in
the freezer section)

While the stock is cooking, make the dumplings: Mix
the ground pork, asparagus, chives, five-spice powder,
tamari or soy sauce, fish sauce, hoisin, black pepper, and
cornstarch until thoroughly combined.

Lay out the gyoza wrappers, covering with a damp kitchen
towel to keep them from drying out while you work. Have
a small bowl of cold water on standby. Holding a wrapper
in one hand, place a teaspoon of mixture in the center.
Dip your fingers into the water and dampen the edges,
then fold in half to create a semicircle, pinching together
at the top. Fold pleats along the edge of the dumpling,
pinching them together as you go to make sure the
wrapper is sealed. Place the dumpling on a baking sheet
lined with parchment paper, cover with a damp kitchen
towel, and continue until all the wrappers have been filled.

Bring the stock to a very gentle simmer. Bring a separate,
very large saucepan, or wide frying pan full of water, to
a boil. Poach the gyoza dumplings for no longer than
5 minutes, flipping over after 2 minutes. Using a slotted
spoon, transfer to four bowls and cover with the hot
umami broth. Serve immediately.

Note: it is not necessary to pleat the gyoza wrappers; you
can simply seal them when folded into half-moon shapes,
if you wish.

Gyoza wrappers should not be refrozen if bought from
the freezer section; if bought fresh, it is fine to freeze the
prepared, uncooked dumplings.

Broth base suitable for freezing

spiced consommé with salmon, buckwheat noodles, and kale

You get a lot of flavor for very little effort here and the ingredients require the simplest preparation. I sometimes serve this with slices of raw salmon only—an elegant and sophisticated entertaining option.

Serves 4 calories 219 (GF if using tamari)

Carbs 23g Sugar 6.5g Protein 16g Fiber 1.1g Fat 6g Sat Fat 1.2g Salt 2.7g

1 onion, peeled and coarsely sliced

1 garlic clove, peeled

⅓ cup tamari or dark soy sauce

1 tablespoon fennel seeds

1 tablespoon coriander seeds

1 star anise

1 cinnamon stick

3 whole cloves

5 black peppercorns

2 tablespoons shaoxing wine

2¼ pounds ripe tomatoes on the vine, coarsely chopped and vines reserved

3½ ounces buckwheat noodles

7 ounces fresh salmon fillet, sliced thinly

3¼ cups kale, chopped

lime wedges, to serve

Place a heavy-bottomed saucepan over high heat and char the sliced onions and garlic clove for 4 to 5 minutes, until they take on a little color.

Add the tamari or soy sauce, fennel seeds, coriander seeds, star anise, cinnamon stick, cloves, peppercorns, shaoxing wine, and 1¾ cups water. Now add the chopped tomatoes, along with their vines. Don't worry if it seems like there are a lot of tomatoes for the amount of liquid—they will reduce in size as they release their juices and soften. Give everything a good stir, place the lid on the saucepan, and simmer over medium heat for 30 minutes.

When ready, mash the juice from the tomatoes using a potato masher. Pass through a very fine strainer and let stand for about 15 minutes. Gently press any remaining liquid from the tomatoes and spices before discarding them.

Cook the noodles according to package instructions. When ready to serve, pour the consommé into a medium saucepan and gently heat to just below boiling point. Add the kale and simmer for 3 to 4 minutes. When ready, divide the kale and warm noodles between four bowls, followed by the slices of salmon. Pour in the broth and serve immediately, with a few wedges of lime.

Consommé only suitable for freezing

turmeric and lemongrass shellfish bisque

This dish makes use of the Turmeric and Lemongrass Paste on page 18, teaming it with coconut water and the heads and shells of fresh jumbo shrimp to make a superbly intense bisque base for the shellfish to be served in. A real showstopper, it's a good option for entertaining as the bisque can be made ahead of time.

Serves 4

Carbs 7g   Sugar 6.5g   Protein 21g   Fiber 0g   Fat 3.2g   Sat Fat 1.6g   Salt 3g

⅓ cup Turmeric and Lemongrass Paste (page 18)
2 cups coconut water
10½ ounces raw jumbo shrimp, heads and shells on
10½ ounces mussels
10½ ounces clams
3 tablespoons fish sauce
juice of 1 lime
2 tablespoons coconut milk
cilantro or parsley, to garnish

Place the turmeric and lemongrass paste, coconut water, and 1½ cups water in a large saucepan and bring to a boil. Remove the heads and shells from the shrimp, add to the stock, and simmer vigorously for 30 minutes. Run a sharp knife down the back of each shrimp, and then use the tip of it to remove the intestinal tract. Rinse under cold water and set aside.

Wash the mussels and clams under plenty of cold water. Discard any that are slightly open but don't close when tapped firmly on the counter. Remove the tough beards protruding from the shells of the mussels along with any barnacles on the surface.

When the stock has reduced by about a third, pass it through a muslin-lined strainer (a cheesecloth will also work). Return to the cleaned-out saucepan and season with the fish sauce and lime juice, adjusting to your taste. Add the coconut milk, followed by the shellfish. Simmer for no longer than 3 to 4 minutes. Serve garnished with chopped cilantro or parsley.

Note: you can freeze leftover coconut milk in tablespoon measures in an ice cube tray to prevent waste (see page 9).

Bisque suitable for freezing without fish

tomato consommé cooler

This is perfect for a sunny summer afternoon sitting in the garden. It is full of fresh, zingy flavors and textures, and there is minimal preparation and literally no cooking involved. Endeavor to make this soup when tomatoes are at the peak of their season from July to October.

Serves 4

Carbs 9.5g   Sugar 8.3g   Protein 3g   Fiber 5.3g   Fat 8g   Sat Fat 1.6g   Salt trace

For the consommé
3¼ pounds ripe tomatoes
1 cucumber, coarsely chopped
2 cups basil
3 teaspoons freshly grated
    horseradish
1 garlic clove, peeled
2 to 3 tablespoons sherry vinegar
juice and zest of 1 lemon
salt, to taste
½ teaspoon black pepper

For the soup
¼ red onion
½ green bell pepper
½ red bell pepper
½ yellow bell pepper
1 celery rib
¼ cucumber
1 unripe avocado

To make the consommé, put the tomatoes, cucumber, basil, horseradish, garlic, sherry vinegar, lemon juice and zest, salt, and pepper into a blender or food processor and process until smooth. You may need to do this in batches.

Line a strainer with some muslin cloth or cheesecloth and place over a large bowl. Pour in the tomato consommé mixture, bring the edges of the muslin or cheesecloth together, and tie with a piece of string.

Place in the fridge and let drain for 6 to 8 hours or overnight. Never squeeze the mixture through the cloth to extract more juice as it will result in a cloudy consommé. This part of the recipe is suitable for freezing.

To serve, finely chop the vegetables and divide evenly between four bowls. Pour in the chilled liquid (straight from the fridge) and serve.

Tips: Instead of discarding the tomato pulp, simmer with a can of chopped tomatoes for 30 minutes, season with salt and pepper, and freeze in batches of about 1 pound for a ready-made pasta sauce.

Using halves of different-colored peppers is for visual purposes; you can, if you wish, use just one type.

tropical consommé with granita

This is a wonderful dessert option when entertaining. Serve in individual bowls, or present as one big chilled punch bowl at a summer barbecue for people to help themselves. If you have any consommé left over, freeze in popsicle molds with the chopped fruit, or use as a base for smoothies.

Serves 4

Carbs 55g   Sugar 55g   Protein 2.5g   Fiber 7g   Fat 1.7g   Sat Fat 0.5g   Salt 0.1g

½ small watermelon
   (approx. 4 pounds), seeded
¼ pineapple (approx. 14 ounces)
¼ cantaloupe (approx.
   1¼ pounds), seeded
1 small papaya (approx.
   9 ounces), seeded and peeled
1 medium mango
seeds of ½ pomegranate
seeds of 2 passion fruit
juice of 1 lime
1 cup coconut water
1 teaspoon vanilla extract

To serve
seeds of remaining
   ½ pomegranate
2 cups pineapple, finely chopped
2 cups melon, finely chopped
2 cups watermelon, seeded and
   finely chopped
granita (see method)
a few sprigs of mint, leaves picked

Peel and coarsely chop all of the fruit. Place in a large bowl along with the lime juice and blend with a hand-held blender until the fruit is all broken down. Alternatively, use a food processor.

Place a strainer lined with muslin or cheesecloth over a large bowl. Pour in the blended fruit, tie the edges of the cloth together, and chill in the fridge overnight.

When the consommé is ready, prepare the granita by placing the leftover fruit pulp into a plastic container with the coconut water and vanilla extract and freeze.

About 30 minutes before you are ready to serve, take the granita from the freezer and let soften a little. This is a good time to prepare the serving fruit. Scrape the surface of the frozen pulp using a fork to make the granita—it will resemble snow-like crystals.

Serve the consommé with the mixed chopped fruit, granita, and a few leaves of fresh mint.

Note: this soup needs to be prepared in advance. Make it the night before you plan to use it, and freeze the granita the following morning. Everything will then be ready by lunchtime, and certainly by the evening.

15-minute soups

Even the keenest of cooks, myself included, will sometimes struggle to fit home cooking into their day. Furthermore, being healthy is often hampered by being busy: when we don't have time to think, to stop, or even to sit down, eating becomes a grab-and-go affair, and we will often wind up making choices we regret.

The soups in this chapter are incredibly easy to whip up, and require little effort, skill, or thought. So even when you're at your most exhausted at the end of a long day, they shouldn't feel unachievable. The Pea, Mint, and Basil and Roasted Red Bell Pepper, Chickpea, and Herb soups, for example, include ingredients that can be kept in the freezer or pantry, meaning you don't have a long shopping list before you can start. One of the simplest recipes in this book, Egg Drop Soup, is about as quick and easy as a dish can be—and surprisingly satisfying too.

Lunch can be the difference between feeling lethargic and slow or fresh and energetic. The right choice can leave you with a fresh lease on life in the middle of the day. The homemade noodle pot recipes in this chapter are designed for you to take to work, and with little more than the addition of boiling hot water, you have a nutritious, filling, satisfying, and generally feel-good lunch on your hands.

It is important to note that the timing for the soups in this chapter starts from the moment you start cooking, not chopping. However, as they are easy and straightforward, the preparation won't be laborious. Also, the first step in most of these recipes is to boil the stock—this is a simple time-saving trick that will have your veggies cooking as soon as they are submerged in liquid.

the quickest tomato soup

Few things can beat a good tomato soup, and having a fail-proof recipe in your repertoire—especially one that only takes minutes to make—will do you good. The recipe accounts for those times when tomatoes are not in season, or when really good ones are hard to come by, but if making it when they are in season, use all fresh.

Serves 4   calories 69 DF GF (V/VE if using vegetable stock)

Carbs 10g   Sugar 9.5g   Protein 1.7g   Fiber 2.7g   Fat 2g   Sat Fat 0.3g   Salt 0.1g

2¼ cups vegetable or chicken stock
2 celery ribs, halved
1 carrot, halved
1 small onion
1 garlic clove
½ tablespoon olive oil
1¼ pounds mixed tomatoes, such as beef, plum, and cherry, coarsely chopped
1 x 14-ounce can plum tomatoes
1 tablespoon red wine vinegar
salt and pepper

In a small saucepan, bring the stock to a boil. Place the celery, carrot, onion, and garlic into a hand-held mini blender and process until coarsely chopped. Transfer to a medium saucepan with the olive oil and 1 tablespoon of water and sauté for a couple of minutes. Add the chopped tomatoes and cook for 2 to 3 minutes longer, followed by the canned tomatoes and stock.

Simmer for 10 minutes. Add the red wine vinegar, process until smooth, and season to taste with salt and pepper.

Serve with Roasted Cherry Tomato Rye Bruschetta (page 80), if you're able to eat gluten. Alternatively, serve the roasted tomatoes as a garnish for this soup.

Tip: As the calorie content of this soup is so low, you can afford to be a little indulgent. Make a cream of tomato soup by adding ⅓ cup cream once the soup has been blended. The soup will then be 105 calories per portion, but won't be dairy-free. You can also add a bunch of basil before blending to create a basil and tomato soup.

roasted cherry tomato rye bruschetta

Nothing beats the punchy flavor of a roasted tomato—it needs little more than some simple seasoning. I have added a splash of sherry vinegar. If you don't have this, balsamic is a good alternative. Equally, if you don't have either this recipe won't suffer, so don't fret.

Serves 4 calories 75

Carbs 13g   Sugar 2.6g   Protein 2.7g   Fiber 2.5g   Fat 0.7g   Sat Fat 0.1g   Salt 0.4g

10½ ounces cherry tomatoes on the vine
1 teaspoon sherry vinegar (optional)
4 thin slices Pumpkin Seed and Prune Rye Soda Bread (page 32)
1 garlic clove, peeled (optional)
basil, to garnish
salt and pepper

Preheat the oven to 475°F or to its highest setting. Place the tomatoes on a baking sheet with the sherry vinegar, if using, and roast for 10 to 15 minutes.

Toast the bread. Rub the garlic, if using, all over each slice. Gently remove the tomatoes from the vine, place four to five on each slice of bread, and use the back of a fork to squash them, releasing their juices. Garnish with some freshly torn basil, salt, and pepper before serving.

homemade lunch noodle pots

Fresh Vegetable Pot with Soy Broth, Chicken, and Pickled Ginger

As this and the other noodle pot recipes are designed to bring to work, each recipe serves one. To avoid wasting leftover ingredients, I'd advise making one recipe a few days in a row. Furthermore, there are no hard-and-fast rules here—use whatever ingredients you have on hand, or simply prefer.

Serves 1 calories 197 DF GF

Carbs 8.5g Sugar 4.2g Protein 14.7g Fiber 2.5g Fat 6.7g Sat Fat 1.3g Salt 2.2g

3 tablespoons tamari or dark soy sauce

½ tablespoon fish sauce

½ tablespoon mirin

juice of ½ lime

3½ ounces or 7 little nests of konnyaku shirataki noodles, rinsed

2½ ounces cooked chicken breast, sliced

1 small bok choy, quartered lengthwise

¼ carrot, julienned or grated

¼ cup kale, chopped

¾ cup red cabbage, thinly sliced

2 sprigs of Thai basil, leaves picked (optional)

2 sprigs of mint, leaves picked

1 red bird's eye chile, thinly sliced (optional)

a few slices of pickled sushi ginger (available in lots of supermarkets, Asian stores, and online)

Mix the tamari or soy sauce, fish sauce, mirin, and lime juice in your soup container, such as a mason jar or small plastic container. Add the noodles and mix well. Now add the remaining ingredients and refrigerate until ready to use. When ready, cover with about 1¼ cups of boiling water, stir everything together, and let stand for 5 minutes before eating.

All noodle pot recipes not suitable for freezing

Salmon and Vegetable Pot with Korean Gochujang Broth

Serves 1 calories 148

Carbs 7g   Sugar 4.2g   Protein 14.7g   Fiber 1.1g   Fat 6.5g   Sat Fat 1.3g   Salt 2.2g

1 tablespoon gochujang

1 tablespoon tamari or light soy sauce

juice of 1 lime

3½ ounces or 7 little nests of konnyaku
    shirataki noodles, rinsed

¼ cup kale, chopped

¼ cup red cabbage, finely sliced

¼ celery rib, finely sliced

1 small scallion, finely sliced

2½ ounces fresh salmon, sliced
    into thin strips

3 to 4 sprigs of cilantro, leaves picked

lime wedge, to serve

Mix the gochujang, tamari or soy sauce, and lime juice in your soup container until it is a smooth paste. Add the noodles and mix well. Now add all of the vegetables, salmon, cilantro, and lime wedge. Refrigerate until ready to use. Remove the lime wedge, cover with about 1¼ cups of boiling water, give a little stir to separate the noodles, and let stand for 5 minutes. Add a squeeze of lime juice before eating.

Walnut Miso Broth Pot with Fennel, Radish, and Enoki Mushrooms

Serves 1 calories 100

Carbs 12g   Sugar 5g   Protein 6g   Fiber 2.6g   Fat 3g   Sat Fat 0.2g   Salt 4g

1 tablespoon Walnut Miso Paste (page 18)

1½ tablespoons tamari or light soy sauce

3½ ounces or 7 little nests of konnyaku
    shirataki noodles, rinsed

½ cup fennel, thinly sliced

2 small radishes, thinly sliced

½ teaspoon lemon juice

2 tablespoons edamame

⅔ cup whole enoki mushrooms (or plain
    button mushrooms, thinly sliced)

1 teaspoon chives, finely chopped

Mix the walnut miso paste with the tamari or soy sauce in the container for your soup. Place the noodles on top and mix well. Slice the fennel and radishes as thinly as possible (a mandolin is best for this) and dress with a little lemon juice. Add to the container along with the edamame, mushrooms, and chives. Refrigerate until ready to use, then cover with 1¼ cups boiling water. Stir gently to separate the noodles and let stand for 5 minutes before eating.

lettuce and gorgonzola with basil

You can play around with the type of lettuce you use here to experiment with the overall flavor. I love to use bitter chicory, which compliments and balances the creaminess of gorgonzola. When I blend this soup I avoid making it completely smooth, as I love the texture of the half blended crunchy lettuce. This is great with the Beet, Chive, and Sumac Buckwheat Tortilla (page 99).

Serves 4 calories 87 GF (V if using vegetable stock)

Carbs 3g   Sugar 2g   Protein 4.5g   Fiber 2.6g   Fat 6g   Sat Fat 3g   Salt 0.6g

3 cups vegetable or chicken stock
1 small leek, finely sliced
1 celery rib, coarsely diced
1 garlic clove, coarsely chopped
½ tablespoon olive oil
1 pound mixed lettuce leaves
    (such as baby gem, chicory,
    romaine), coarsely chopped
⅓ cup gorgonzola cheese
1¼ cups basil
juice of 1 lemon
salt and pepper

Place the stock in a saucepan and bring to a boil.

Sauté the leek, celery, and garlic in the olive oil and 1 tablespoon water for 4 to 5 minutes, until slightly softened. Add the lettuce and boiling stock. Don't worry that the stock doesn't cover the lettuce—as it heats the water, the lettuce will wilt. Use the back of a wooden spoon to push the leaves down into the liquid. Simmer for about 8 minutes.

Add the gorgonzola and basil and blend, leaving a little texture. Stir in the lemon juice, season to taste, and serve.

pea, mint, and basil

This soup is all about the vibrant flavors of the peas and fresh herbs, and they need little more than an onion to get things going. For an Asian twist, add ¼ teaspoon of chile flakes when cooking the onion, and substitute basil with Thai basil. If you have time, this soup is delicious served with Peppered Sweet Potato Chips (page 45).

Serves 4

Carbs 13g   Sugar 12g   Protein 23g   Fiber 5g   Fat 3.3g   Sat Fat 0.7g   Salt 6.8g

2½ cups vegetable stock
I small onion, chopped
½ tablespoon olive oil
5 cups frozen peas
1¼ cups basil, leaves picked
I cup mint, leaves picked
salt and pepper

Bring the stock to a boil in a saucepan.

Sauté the onion in the olive oil and I tablespoon water for 2 to 3 minutes. Add the peas, followed by the boiling stock, and cook for 10 minutes. Add the herbs, blend until smooth, and season to taste.

roasted red bell pepper, chickpea, and herb

Many of the ingredients in this soup can be kept in your pantry for when you need a convenient and tasty supper. Only buy roasted red bell peppers preserved in water and vinegar, not oil, and splurge on a good-quality jar. Remember, they are the hero of your soup, and cheaper versions can have an almost unpalatable vinegary flavor. I have used tomato sauce as the base for this soup as the sweetness of the peppers calls for an acidic counterbalance.

Serves 4   (GF if using GF stock cube)

Carbs 22g   Sugar 7.5g   Protein 8g   Fiber 10g   Fat 10g   Sat Fat 0.6g   Salt 1.9g

2¾ cups tomato sauce

1 vegetable bouillon cube

1 small red onion, finely chopped

2 garlic cloves, finely chopped

1 medium red bell pepper, diced

½ teaspoon smoked paprika

½ tablespoon olive oil

1 x 16-ounce jar roasted red bell peppers, drained and chopped into bite-sized pieces

1 x 14-ounce can of chickpeas, drained and rinsed

large bunch of basil, coarsely chopped

2 sprigs of thyme, leaves picked

2 sprigs marjoram, leaves picked and chopped

salt and pepper

Place the tomato sauce, bouillon cube, and ¾ cup water in a small saucepan and bring to a boil.

Meanwhile, in another saucepan, sauté the red onion, garlic, red bell pepper, and smoked paprika in the oil and 1 tablespoon of water, for 5 minutes. Add more water if the mixture sticks to the pan.

Add the roasted red bell peppers, chickpeas, and boiling sauce. Simmer for 10 minutes.

When ready, season with salt if you feel you need it— you may not after using the bouillon cube—and lots of black pepper. Stir in the herbs and serve.

korean kimchi with tofu

Native to Korea, kimchi is basically fermented vegetables, usually cabbage, and is deliciously spicy and sour. Although you can make your own, I tend to buy it from my local Asian supermarket or online.

Serves 4 calories 164 GF V

Carbs 5g   Sugar 4g   Protein 8.5g   Fiber 4.5g   Fat 11g   Sat Fat 2.5g   Salt 1.7g

14 ounces cabbage kimchi

½ tablespoon sesame oil, plus extra to serve

1 medium onion, finely chopped

2 garlic cloves, finely chopped

2 tablespoons gochujang (Korean chile paste)

1 tablespoon mirin

5½ ounces firm tofu, cut into ¾-inch cubes

4 large free-range egg yolks (optional)

2 scallions, sliced

1 tablespoon black sesame seeds

Remove the kimchi from its packaging and squeeze out any juice, reserving for later.

Heat the sesame oil in a medium saucepan and sauté the onion, garlic, and kimchi over medium heat for 3 to 4 minutes, adding a splash of water if necessary.

Stir in the gochujang, mirin, and reserved kimchi juice, followed by 4 cups of water, and bring to a boil. Reduce to a simmer and cook gently for 10 minutes. Remove from the heat and add the tofu.

Serve in bowls, with an egg yolk (if using) resting on top, and garnish with scallions, black sesame seeds, and a drizzle of sesame oil.

Tip: to make this soup vegan, simply leave out the egg yolk.

Not suitable for freezing

fennel, celery, and cucumber broth with cilantro, mint, and lime pesto

This soup is all about invigorating, sharp, clean, and crisp flavors. Next to no cooking is required, as its preparation is simple. A spoonful of the cilantro, mint, and lime pesto stirred through the broth makes it even more special! The pesto is best made using a mortar and pestle. A one-tablespoon serving is sufficient for one person adorning a soup and any leftovers can be frozen in an ice cube tray for use at a later time.

Serves 4

Carbs 1.7g   Sugar 2g   Protein 2g   Fiber 2g   Fat 0.7g   Sat Fat 0g   Salt trace

5 cups vegetable stock
1 small fennel bulb
4 celery ribs
2 garlic cloves, peeled
8 black peppercorns
1 sprig of mint
½ large cucumber
(approx. 5½ ounces)

For the Cilantro, Mint, and Lime Pesto (17 calories per serving: makes ½ cup; serves 8)
¾ cup mint, leaves picked
1¼ cups cilantro
1 garlic clove, peeled
2 tablespoons whole almonds
1½ tablespoons olive oil
juice of 2 limes
salt and pepper

Boil the vegetable stock in a medium saucepan. Quarter the fennel, remove the tough outer layer, and add this to the stock along with 1 rib of celery, the garlic, peppercorns, and mint. Allow to simmer while you prepare the vegetables.

If you have a mandolin, or a food processor with a slice attachment, thinly slice the fennel quarters, remaining celery, and cucumber. Otherwise do this by hand.

Strain the stock, return to the pan, and reduce the heat so that it is just below a simmer. Add the sliced vegetables and cook for 5 minutes.

Meanwhile, make the pesto: Coarsely chop the herbs and add to the mortar with the garlic and almonds. Pound until you have a coarse paste. Add the oil and lime juice, mix well, and season with salt and pepper.

When the soup is ready, top with a spoonful of pesto. Serve immediately.

Soup not suitable for freezing

egg drop soup

When I think of fast food, I think of eggs. Nothing can be prepared more quickly, in so many different ways, and be so utterly satisfying and good for you. This soup is the essence of simplicity. You can flavor the stock if you wish, allowing it to simmer for a few minutes with a few cloves, some star anise, and a cinnamon stick. You could also stir through a few tablespoons of sweet white miso. To make this for one, use about 1¼ cups stock and 1 whole egg.

Serves 4   (GF if using homemade chicken stock; V if using vegetable stock)

Carbs 1.7g   Sugar 0.6g   Protein 6g   Fiber 0.2g   Fat 5g   Sat Fat 1.3g   Salt 0.2g

5 cups chicken or vegetable stock,
    preferably homemade
1 teaspoon cornstarch
3 large free-range eggs
3 scallions, sliced
salt and pepper

Bring the chicken stock to a boil and reduce the heat so that it is barely simmering—it is important not to pour the eggs into a boiling stock. Taste and season to your liking in order to create a strong base for the remaining ingredients.

Mix the cornstarch with a little water to form a smooth paste and then whisk in the eggs. Season with salt and pepper.

Pour the eggs into the stock in a very thin steady stream using a whisk to gently incorporate them. As soon as the eggs have been added, remove from the heat and let stand for a minute or two. The soup will have a slightly curdled effect, but this is how it should look, so don't worry. Serve immediately, garnished with scallions.

Not suitable for freezing

broccoli and ginger with yogurt, cucumber, and mint

Both broccoli and ginger are packed with antioxidants, and each boasts its own collection of vitamins and nutrients to make this soup a real star. There is a very gentle heat from the chile and ginger, which is beautifully counterbalanced by the addition of some cooling cucumber, yogurt, and mint.

Serves 4 calories 103 GF

Carbs 10g   Sugar 6.5g   Protein 7g   Fiber 5.5g   Fat 3g   Sat Fat 1.7g   Salt 0.2g

¾ cup coconut water

3 cups boiling vegetable stock

4 scallions, tough green tips removed and coarsely chopped

1 garlic clove, coarsely chopped

3 tablespoons ginger, peeled and grated

1 green chile, seeds removed and coarsely chopped

½ teaspoon garam masala

½ tablespoon coconut oil

1¼-pound head of broccoli, broken into very small florets and stalks coarsely chopped

salt and pepper

To serve

2 tablespoons plain yogurt

¼ cucumber, seeded and finely grated or chopped

a few sprigs of mint, leaves picked and finely chopped

Add the coconut water to the stock and bring to a boil.

Sauté the scallions, garlic, ginger, chile, and garam masala in the coconut oil and 1 tablespoon of water over medium heat for 2 to 3 minutes, stirring occasionally.

Add the broccoli, followed by the boiling stock and coconut water. Turn the heat right up so that it boils quickly, then reduce the heat and simmer for 8 minutes.

Blend the soup until smooth and season to taste. Serve topped with yogurt, cucumber, and mint.

mushroom soup with a kick

This spicy, salty, earthy soup is refreshingly unpredictable. It has a real depth of flavor that bounces around your palate and leaves behind a smacking warmth that will have you chile lovers coming back for more (if you are not a spice lover, feel free to leave out the chiles). Don't fuss over chopping the mushrooms, simply tear them into the pot to save time.

Serves 4   (V/VE if using vegetable stock)

Carbs 4g   Sugar 3.5g   Protein 6g   Fiber 2g   Fat 2g   Sat Fat 0.3g   Salt 2.2g

3 cups vegetable, mushroom, or beef stock

1 red onion, sliced

2 garlic cloves, coarsely sliced

2 bay leaves

3 sprigs of thyme, leaves picked

2 sprigs of rosemary, leaves picked and coarsely chopped

1 small red chile, coarsely chopped (seeds removed if you prefer less heat)

½ tablespoon olive oil

1½ pounds crimini mushrooms, torn into chunks

2 tablespoons tamari or light soy sauce

salt and pepper

Bring the stock to a boil. Sauté the onion, garlic, bay leaves, thyme, rosemary, and chile in the olive oil and 1 tablespoon water over medium heat for 5 minutes.

Add the mushrooms and stock and boil for 10 minutes. Remove the bay leaves, then add the tamari or soy sauce and blend until smooth. Season to taste. You won't need much salt, if any, as the soy sauce is naturally salty.

Note: mushrooms can be reluctant to break down so you need to be patient, if using an immersion blender, to achieve a smooth consistency.

buckwheat tortillas done three ways

When we think soup, big chunks of crusty bread come to mind as an accompaniment. These flavorful buckwheat tortillas provide the same bit of substance without weighing you down the way that bread can. You can slice them and use them to scoop up soup or fill them like a wrap and serve alongside a soup for a more filling meal. Feel free to experiment.

Walnut Miso and Scallion

Serves 4

Carbs 17g   Sugar 1g   Protein 2g   Fiber 0.7g   Fat 4g   Sat Fat 0.3g   Salt 0.3g

⅔ cup buckwheat flour
I large free-range egg white
2½ tablespoons Walnut Miso
   Paste (page 18)
3 scallions, finely sliced
canola oil, for frying
salt and pepper

Whisk the flour, egg white, and ¾ cups water until you have a smooth batter, similar in consistency to half-and-half. Add the remaining ingredients and season generously.

Heat a skillet or heavy-bottomed frying pan and brush with a little canola oil. Pour in a ladleful of batter and spread around the pan. Cook for 3 to 4 minutes on each side and repeat with the remaining batter. Serve with Pea, Mint, and Basil Soup (page 87) or Broccoli and Ginger Soup (page 96).

Beet, Chive, and Sumac

Serves 4

Carbs 16g   Sugar 1g   Protein 2.7g   Fiber 0.9g   Fat 3g   Sat Fat 0.2g   Salt 0.1g

⅔ cup buckwheat flour
I large free-range egg white
I raw beet, grated
1½ tablespoons chives, finely
   chopped
½ teaspoon sumac
canola oil, for frying
salt and pepper

Follow the instructions above.

Serve with Lettuce and Gorgonzola Soup with Basil (page 85) or Fennel, Celery, and Cucumber Broth with Cilantro, Mint, and Lime Pesto (page 92)

Zucchini, Feta Cheese, and Thyme

Serves 4   calories 116 GF V

Carbs 16g   Sugar 0.5g   Protein 3.6g   Fiber 0.8g   Fat 4g   Sat Fat 0.9g   Salt 0.2g

⅔ cup buckwheat flour
1 large free-range egg white
1 small zucchini, grated
2 tablespoons feta cheese
4 sprigs of thyme, leaves picked
canola oil, for frying
salt and pepper

Follow the instructions on page 99.

Serve with Chunky Zucchini and Dill with Shrimp (page 102), Mushroom Soup with a Kick (page 98), or Roasted Red Bell Pepper, Chickpea, and Herb (page 88).

A note on buckwheat flour

This flour is gluten-free and has a deliciously delicate, earthy flavor. It's worth keeping in the pantry, as the tortillas won't work or taste the same using all-purpose flour. It's available in big supermarkets, health-food stores, and online.

chunky zucchini and dill with shrimp

This soup boasts a lot of flavor for the little time and effort it takes to make. It's important to use fresh shrimp here and even more important not to overcook them.

Serves 4 calories 88 DF GF

Carbs 4.5g   Sugar 3g   Protein 11g   Fiber 2.5g   Fat 2.5g   Sat Fat 0.5g   Salt 0.3g

2½ cups vegetable or chicken stock
½ tablespoon olive oil
1 medium leek, halved and sliced into half-moons, about ¼-inch thick
3 medium zucchini, halved and sliced into half-moons about ¼-inch thick
½ teaspoon chile flakes (optional)
zest and juice of ½ lime
2 cups dill sprigs, fronds picked and chopped
6 ounces raw shelled shrimp
salt and pepper

Boil the stock in a medium saucepan. Heat the oil in another saucepan and sauté the leek and zucchini with 1 tablespoon water for about 4 minutes, stirring occasionally.

Add the boiling stock and simmer for another 5 minutes. Add the chile flakes and lime zest and juice. Remove half of the soup and blend with half of the dill until smooth. Return to the saucepan, add the shrimp, and cook for no more than 3 minutes, until they have turned pink.

Just before serving, stir through the remaining dill. Season to taste and serve immediately.

Not suitable for freezing

Note: serve with Zucchini, Feta Cheese, and Thyme or Walnut Miso and Scallion buckwheat tortillas (pages 99–100).

grains and pulses

The variety of grains and pulses available to us is vast and at times overwhelming. However, they are without doubt one of the healthiest food groups. Each has its own distinctive, sometimes delicate, at other times more punchy flavor. They are full of good things such as protein and fiber, give a slow release of energy, fill us up for longer, are generally easy to cook, and are mostly very affordable. Furthermore, their uses reach far beyond the soup recipes in this book, making them a sensible pantry staple: teamed with wild mushrooms, pearl barley makes a great risotto; mixed with some olive oil, tahini, garlic, and lemon, chickpeas will transform into a decadent hummus; and quinoa is a great all-around ingredient, as comfortable in granola and cakes as it is in salads, soups, and stews.

This chapter showcases how versatile grains and pulses can be, ranging from Mexican Posole Verde Soup to the more traditional Caramelized Onion, Pearl Barley, and Cavolo Nero soup. Freekeh is a perfect demonstration of how flavorful a grain can be, boasting aromas and flavors not dissimilar to smoky bacon. Cannellini beans make a creamy smooth-textured soup base for pomegranate and tahini-roasted broccoli (see page 118), while they can also be served as a garnish, creating texture and interest. Chickpeas are converted into deep purple roasted jewels for a simple but delicious watercress soup.

The recipes in this chapter are among the most filling in the book, and generally have a calorie content closer to the 300 mark. They work brilliantly as a more substantial meal option, and will not only fill you up, but will keep you going too. These are a fantastic example of how, as we would say in Ireland, "There is eatin' and drinkin' in that soup."

carrot, rhubarb, and yellow lentil

Carrot and rhubarb may seem like an odd combination, but the sour rhubarb complements the sweet carrots and the result is a rather lovely, subtle flavor of both.

Serves 4   (V/VE if using vegetable stock)

Carbs 20g   Sugar 10.5g   Protein 12g   Fiber 9g   Fat 2.5g   Sat Fat 0.6g   Salt 0.4g

2 to 3 large shallots, finely chopped

2½ tablespoons ginger, finely chopped

½ tablespoon olive oil

1¼ pounds carrots, peeled and coarsely diced (approx. 4 cups)

⅓ cup yellow split lentils

1 star anise

2 cardamom pods

3 cups vegetable or chicken stock

2 cups pink rhubarb, coarsely chopped

salt and pepper

Sauté the shallot and ginger in the olive oil and 1 tablespoon of water for about 5 minutes, adding a splash more water if necessary.

Add the carrots, lentils, star anise, cardamom, and stock. Bring to a boil and cook for 15 minutes. Add the rhubarb and cook for another 10 minutes, or until the carrots are tender.

When ready, remove the spices and blend until smooth. Add a little more water or stock if the soup is too thick. Season to taste and serve with Health-kick Crackers or Savory Granola (page 108).

Note: a spoonful of sweet white miso would add another flavor dimension to this soup, or add a drizzle of Cilantro, Mint, and Lime Pesto (page 92).

health-kick crackers and savory granola

The crunch of a cracker, and the texture provided by a sprinkling of savory granola can really transform a soup. Both are really nutritious, and you could add a variety of flavors too if you are feeling a bit fancy. Herbs such as rosemary and thyme work well, as do all dried spices.

Makes 25 crackers

Carbs 1.8g   Sugar 0.1g   Protein 1.4g   Fiber 0.7g   Fat 2.4g   Sat Fat 0.4g   Salt 0.2g

1 cup pumpkin seeds
1 cup sunflower seeds
⅓ cup golden flaxseed
¼ cup black sesame seeds
2 teaspoons sea salt
1¼ cups jumbo oats
2 tablespoons tahini
2 soft pitted prunes

2 large baking sheets

Preheat the oven to 300°F. Place all the seeds, the sea salt, and ½ cup of the jumbo oats in a medium bowl. Using a mini hand-held blender, process the remaining oats to a fine powder. Add to the bowl with the rest of the ingredients and mix well.

Blend the tahini, prunes, and about ½ cup of water until smooth. Mix with the dry ingredients until you have sticky dough.

Divide the mixture in half and roll out each half as thinly as possible between two sheets of parchment paper.

Place the rolled-out mixture on two baking sheets and remove the top layer of parchment paper. Bake for 20 to 25 minutes, until dry, crisp, and golden brown. Let cool completely. Break one batch into 25 crackers and crumble the other to make a savory garnish for soups and salads.

Store for up to 2 weeks in an airtight container.

mexican posole verde (celebration soup)

There are times when soup deserves its place center stage, and I can think of nothing nicer than sitting down to a big pot of this vibrant and invigorating soup, with all kinds of garnishes served alongside. It is perfect for a celebration! For a list of suppliers for ingredients in this recipe, see page 156.

Serves 6 calories 208 GF

Carbs 17g Sugar 7g Protein 18g Fiber 5g Fat 6.5g Sat Fat 2g Salt 0.7g

2 small chicken breasts (approx. 10½ ounces)
1¾ cups chicken stock
1¼ pounds tomatillos, papery skins removed, washed and halved (alternatively use canned)
5 scallions
2 jalapeño peppers
2 poblano chiles
5 garlic cloves
juice of 2 limes
2½ cups cilantro
12 ounces canned hominy (approx. 2 cups)

For the garnishes
⅔ cup avocado, diced and dressed with a little lemon or lime juice
4 pink radishes, finely sliced
½ cup cilantro
small handful of cherry tomatoes, quartered
3 tablespoons sour cream

Place the chicken breasts in a saucepan and cover with the chicken stock. Bring to a boil, reduce to a simmer, and poach for 10 to 12 minutes. Remove the chicken and let cool, then slice thinly. Set the stock aside to cool.

Place the tomatillos, scallions, jalapeño peppers, poblano chiles, garlic, lime juice, cilantro, and 1¼ cups of the hominy in a blender with the reserved chicken stock and pulse until very smooth. You may need to do this in batches. You can make the soup up to this point a day in advance and keep refrigerated.

When you are ready to serve, prepare your chosen garnishes. Pour the soup into a large saucepan, add the remaining ¾ cup of hominy, gently bring to a boil, and quickly reduce the heat. It's important not to overheat or boil it as the color will quickly diminish. When ready, taste for seasoning and bring to the table with a ladle for people to help themselves. Serve with the garnishes and sliced chicken.

Tip: Other garnishes you can also choose are scallions, finely chopped red onion, corn, lime wedges, Health-kick Crackers, or Savory Granola (opposite).

greek chicken and lemon with dill

Native to Greece and known as Avgolemono, this soup uses egg yolks as a thickening agent and to create richness. It is a masterclass in simplicity, but for it to work you need to use the best ingredients you can get your hands on.

Serves 4

Carbs 19g   Sugar 1.3g   Protein 29g   Fiber 1.2g   Fat 11g   Sat Fat 3g   Salt 0.6g

4 cups chicken stock
1¼ pounds chicken thighs, bone in and skin removed (about 5 chicken thighs; approx. 10 ounces meat when cooked)
¾ cup orzo pasta
2 free-range egg yolks
juice of 1 lemon (about 2 tablespoons)
3 sprigs of fresh dill
salt and pepper

Bring the chicken stock to a boil and add the chicken. Reduce to a simmer and cook for 12 minutes, skimming any fat that rises to the surface. Add the pasta after 4 minutes.

After 12 minutes, when the chicken is cooked, remove and let cool slightly. Reduce the heat so that the stock and orzo are just below simmering point. Whisk 3 to 4 tablespoons of the hot stock into the egg yolks (don't be tempted to add the eggs straight to the soup—they will curdle), then add to the stock and stir through.

Cook for 3 to 4 minutes over very gentle heat—you don't want to boil the soup now as it will separate. As you stir the soup it will thicken slightly, becoming similar in consistency to heavy cream. Add the lemon juice and season to taste. Shred the chicken, discarding the bones, and add to the soup, along with the dill, and serve immediately.

Note: this soup is best eaten fresh.

Not suitable for freezing

roasted tomato, harissa, and pomegranate black bean

This is a blend of sharp pomegranate, sour tomatoes, and fiery, aromatic harissa all brought together under a blanket of silken black beans. Use your own spice gauge for this soup—one whole tablespoon of rose harissa will give you a considerable smack of heat, so only use half a tablespoon if you prefer a more delicate spicing.

Serves 4   (V/VE if using vegetable stock)

calories 128 DF GF

Carbs 19.5g   Sugar 8.7g   Protein 6g   Fiber 7.7g   Fat 1.2g   Sat Fat 0.2g   Salt 0.2g

1 teaspoon cumin seeds

1 teaspoon coriander seeds

1 tablespoon rose harissa (use regular harissa if you can't find this)

1½ tablespoons pomegranate molasses

1 tablespoon tomato paste

3 garlic cloves, finely chopped

2 teaspoons chopped fresh oregano (use dried if you can't find fresh)

juice of 1 lime

½ teaspoon black pepper

1¼ pounds tomatoes on the vine, each cut into eight wedges

1¾ cups beef or vegetable stock

1 x 14-ounce can black beans

2 tablespoons sour cream (optional—dish won't be dairy-free or vegan if used)

fresh pomegranate seeds to garnish (optional)

Preheat the oven to 400°F. Place a small frying pan over medium heat and toast the cumin and coriander seeds for a couple of minutes, or until fragrant and just beginning to pop. Grind to a fine powder in a mortar and pestle.

Mix the ground spices, harissa, pomegranate molasses, tomato paste, garlic, oregano, lime juice, and black pepper in a medium bowl with 1 tablespoon water. Add the tomatoes, coat with the marinade, transfer to a shallow ovenproof casserole dish or Dutch oven and roast for 30 minutes, checking and turning halfway through.

Shortly before the tomatoes are ready, bring the stock to a boil. Remove the dish from the oven and add the black beans, along with their juices, and the boiling stock. Give everything a good stir, cover with a lid or tight layer of foil, return to the oven, and cook for 15 minutes.

When ready, taste for seasoning and serve with sour cream and fresh pomegranate seeds to garnish.

Garnish not suitable for freezing

fava bean, freekeh, and smoked mackerel

Freekeh packs a real punch of flavor. The grains are very absorbent, so you may have to add a little more water or stock as you cook. I mostly use frozen fava beans for this, but, if they are in season, it is nice to use fresh. Peeling them is worth the effort, but if you are strapped for time the world won't come crashing down if you leave them like they are!

Serves 4 calories 180

Carbs 16g   Sugar 4.6g   Protein 8g   Fiber 5g   Fat 8g   Sat Fat 1.6g   Salt 0.5g

2 to 3 large shallots, finely chopped
1 garlic clove, finely chopped
2 carrots, diced
½ tablespoon olive oil
¼ cup freekeh, rinsed
3½ ounces smoked mackerel, skin removed
1½ cups frozen fava beans, defrosted and skinned
2 tablespoons dill (optional)
salt and pepper
1 lemon, cut into four wedges, to serve

Sauté the shallots, garlic, and carrots in the olive oil and 1 tablespoon of water for 10 minutes, stirring occasionally. Add a splash more water if the vegetables stick to the pan. Add the freekeh along with 4 cups of water. Bring to a boil and simmer with the lid on for 20 to 25 minutes.

If the grains have absorbed too much of the water, add a little more to achieve a brothy consistency and bring back to a boil. Flake the smoked mackerel into the soup in bite-sized pieces and simmer for about 5 minutes. Add the fava beans, then remove from the heat. You only want to heat the fava beans through, to keep them as fresh, green, and crunchy as possible. Stir in the chopped dill if using, check for seasoning, and serve with a wedge of lemon.

Note: if you can't find freekeh, use brown rice instead. Check cooking times on the package and use vegetable or chicken stock instead of water.

Not suitable for freezing

A note on freekeh

Freekeh boasts three times the amount of fiber and protein as brown rice and has a smoky, almost bacon-like flavor. It is made from early harvested wheat, which results in a grain that is slightly green in color. So assertive is its flavor, that when used in soups, there is no need for stock. It is also a fantastic base for salads. You will most likely find it in supermarket aisles, but, failing that, health-food stores are almost certain to sell it.

caramelized onion, pearl barley, and cavolo nero

Onions find their way into almost all of our kitchens, but will rarely be the star of their own show. Slowly sautéed, as they are here, they change into a silky, robustly flavored, caramelized version of themselves—addictively rich, succulent, earthy, and sweet. This soup epitomizes the beauty that lies in some of our most everyday ingredients.

Serves 4 calories 225 DF GF (V/VE if using Mushroom Stock and vegetarian Worcestershire sauce)

Carbs 33g   Sugar 19g   Protein 12g   Fiber 6.5g   Fat 3.6g   Sat Fat 0.5g   Salt 0.6g

2 pounds onions (unpeeled weight)
½ tablespoon olive oil
2 tablespoons Worcestershire sauce
2 cups beef stock (or use Mushroom Stock, page 16)
1 tablespoon finely chopped rosemary
1 tablespoon finely chopped thyme
1 tablespoon finely chopped marjoram (optional)
¼ cup pearl barley
1¼ cups unsweetened soy milk
1 cup cavolo nero (savoy cabbage will suffice), shredded
salt and pepper

Halve, peel, and trim the onions. If you have a food processor, use the slicing blade to prepare them, otherwise, thinly slice by hand. Add to a large heavy-bottomed casserole dish or frying pan along with the oil, Worcestershire sauce, and 2 tablespoons of the beef stock. Give the onions a good stir, then cover and sauté for 50 minutes, adding the herbs halfway through. Check regularly, stirring each time. Add a splash of beef stock or water if the onions stick to the pan. It is important not to burn them.

Meanwhile, rinse the pearl barley under cold water until the water runs clear. Place in a medium saucepan, cover with 1 cup water, and simmer for 25 to 30 minutes. If the barley has absorbed all the water before it is fully cooked, simply add a little more water. When ready, drain and set aside.

When the onions are soft and a deep brown color, add the stock and pearl barley and simmer for 10 minutes. Add the soy milk, along with the cavolo nero, and heat until just at boiling point. Generously season before serving.

cannellini bean with pomegranate and tahini-roasted broccoli

The base of this soup is very subtle—velvety smooth and light—providing a delicate base for the more intensely flavored roasted broccoli garnish, salty from the soy sauce and sour from pomegranate molasses. The broccoli in this recipe also makes a perfect addition to salads.

Serves 4   calories 215   DF   GF (V/VE if using vegetable stock)

Carbs 23g   Sugar 10g   Protein 11g   Fiber 11.5g   Fat 6g   Sat Fat 1g   Salt 1g

1½ tablespoons tahini

¾ tablespoon pomegranate molasses

2 tablespoons tamari or light soy sauce

14-ounce head of broccoli, broken into small florets, stalks coarsely chopped

½ tablespoon olive oil

1 small onion, finely chopped

1 garlic clove, finely sliced

1 small carrot, finely chopped

2 tablespoons ginger, peeled and grated

¼ teaspoon chile flakes

1 x 14-ounce can cannellini beans, drained

3½ cups vegetable or chicken stock

¼ cup pomegranate seeds, to garnish

Preheat the oven to 350°F. Mix ½ tablespoon tahini with the pomegranate molasses and tamari or soy sauce in a medium bowl. Add the broccoli florets and thoroughly coat. Transfer to a lined baking sheet and roast for 8 to 10 minutes. Keep a close eye to make sure they don't burn.

Heat the oil in a medium saucepan and sauté the onion, garlic, carrot, ginger, chile flakes, and broccoli stalks for 3 to 4 minutes. Add a splash of water if the vegetables stick to the pan. Add the cannellini beans and stock, bring to a boil, and simmer for about 10 minutes, or until the carrot is tender.

Blend the soup, with the remaining tablespoon of tahini, and season to taste. Serve garnished with the roasted broccoli and a scattering of fresh pomegranate seeds.

roasted eggplant and wild rice

It is easy to find both red rice and wild rice in supermarkets and health-food stores. Both are delicious grains of rice, much tastier and more satisfying, I think, than white and brown varieties. To mix them go for an 8:2 ratio of red to wild. Some supermarkets do the work for you and sell it in packages already mixed.

Serves 4

Carbs 36g   Sugar 17g   Protein 6g   Fiber 6g   Fat 4g   Sat Fat 3g   Salt 1.4g

4 medium tomatoes on the vine, coarsely chopped

2 stalks of lemongrass, coarsely chopped

5 scallions, coarsely chopped

1 red chile, seeded if you prefer milder spice

3 tablespoons ginger, peeled and coarsely chopped

2 garlic cloves, peeled

juice of 1 lime

1½ tablespoons tamari or light soy sauce

3½ cups coconut water

½ cup mix of red rice and wild rice

2 eggplant (approx. 1¼ pounds)

1 tablespoon coconut oil

1 teaspoon cumin powder

¾ cup cilantro, coarsely chopped

salt and pepper

Blend the tomatoes, lemongrass, scallions, chile, ginger, garlic, lime juice, and tamari or soy sauce until as smooth as possible. A blender is best for this—if using a hand-held immersion blender, process for a good few minutes.

Transfer to a saucepan, along with the coconut water and ¾ cup water. Bring to a boil. Meanwhile, wash and rinse the rice. Add to the simmering liquid and cook for 25 minutes with the lid on. Some froth may rise to the surface from the paste and the rice—simply skim this off.

Preheat the oven to 400°F. Cut the eggplant into ¾-inch cubes. Melt the coconut oil if solid and pour over the eggplant, mixing well. Transfer to a large baking sheet and season with the cumin powder, salt, and pepper. Roast for about 25 minutes, turning halfway through and keeping a close eye to make sure they don't burn.

When ready, remove from the oven, check for seasoning, and stir through the chopped cilantro. Serve the soup with a handful of eggplant placed on top.

Not suitable for freezing

beets with tarragon buckwheat

Beets can take a ferociously long time to cook, so I grate it prior
to cooking to allow the heat to penetrate much quicker, enabling this
soup to be whipped up in no time. As it is a fruit seed rather than a grain,
buckwheat is gluten-free. It is also high in protein and soluble fiber,
requires no overnight soaking, and cooks quickly!

Serves 4

calories 147   DF   GF   V   VE

Carbs 27g   Sugar 9g   Protein 4g   Fiber 4g   Fat 1.5g   Sat Fat 0.2g   Salt 0.3g

½ cup raw or unroasted
   buckwheat
generous pinch of salt
1 teaspoon olive oil
1 medium onion, coarsely diced
1 garlic clove, finely sliced
½ teaspoon fennel seeds,
   ground in a mortar and pestle
3 medium beets, approximately
   1 pound unpeeled weight
1 tablespoon plus 1 teaspoon
   sherry vinegar
3 cups vegetable stock
¾ cup tarragon, leaves picked
   and coarsely chopped
1 teaspoon English mustard
black pepper

Rinse the buckwheat in a strainer under cold water and
transfer to a saucepan with about ⅔ cup cold water and
a generous pinch of salt. Simmer with the lid on for
8 to 10 minutes until tender. Drain and run under cold
water to stop the cooking process. Set aside in the strainer
to ensure all excess liquid drains from the seeds.

Gently heat the olive oil and add the onion, garlic, and
ground fennel along with 1 tablespoon water. Sweat, with
the lid on, for 5 minutes, stirring regularly. Add a splash
more water if the onion sticks to the pan.

Peel and coarsely grate the beets and add to the saucepan
with the tablespoon of sherry vinegar and stock. Bring to a
boil, reduce to a simmer, and cook for 15 to 20 minutes,
until the beets are tender.

Meanwhile pound the tarragon, mustard, and teaspoon of
sherry vinegar in a mortar and pestle to a smooth paste.
Season to taste and stir through the buckwheat. Set aside.

When the soup is ready, blend until smooth and season to
taste. If the beets are particularly sweet, a good grinding of
pepper may be needed to create a good balance. Serve the
soup, topped with the tarragon dressed buckwheat, and
Beet Chips (page 45).

aromatic dhal with mustard seeds and curry leaves

Sri Lanka gave me some of my most memorable food experiences. Dining in local hole-in-the-wall style restaurants I ate rice and curry almost every day. It was always served with Dhal and I was fascinated by the levels of flavor and texture in a dish made with something as basic as lentils. This recipe includes many ingredients, which can be intimidating, but you will not be disappointed.

Serves 4 calories 250

Carbs 38g   Sugar 5g   Protein 17g   Fiber 5.5g   Fat 2g   Sat Fat 0.2g   Salt 0.1g

¾ cup yellow lentils

¾ cup red lentils

I cinnamon stick

3 cardamom pods

2 cloves

I onion, thinly sliced

3 garlic cloves, finely chopped

I tablespoon coconut oil

½ teaspoon each of turmeric, ground cumin, ground cinnamon, and garam masala

2 tablespoons fresh ginger, peeled and grated

I to 2 green bird's eye chiles, finely chopped

3 medium tomatoes, coarsely chopped

I tablespoon mustard seeds

20 to 25 curry leaves

lime wedges, to serve

Rinse the lentils under cold water until the water runs clear. Place in a saucepan with the cinnamon stick, cardamom pods, and cloves and cover with 2 cups cold water. Bring to a boil, cover, and simmer for 25 to 30 minutes, stirring occasionally. If necessary, add some water while cooking, but only a little at a time.

Meanwhile, gently cook the onion with the garlic in ½ tablespoon coconut oil and I tablespoon water. Cook for 10 to 15 minutes, stirring regularly, until browned and caramelized, adding a splash more water if necessary. Add the ground spices, followed by the ginger, chiles, and tomatoes. Cook until the tomatoes have broken down and surrendered their juices—about 10 minutes. Use a potato masher to break up any remaining chunks.

Remove the spices from the lentils and beat or whisk for a few minutes to a smooth soup consistency, adding a little more water or stock if it is too thick. Pour in the spiced tomato mixture and stir through. Wipe the frying pan clean and add the remaining coconut oil, followed by the mustard seeds and curry leaves. Cook, stirring, until the mustard seeds begin to pop. Stir through the soup and serve with lime wedges.

zucchini and feta puy lentil with black olives, capers, and cherry tomatoes

While driving around Santorini with my husband, we'd stop to sample local dishes in shabby little restaurants. In the scalding heat, we ate mostly salads, effortlessly thrown together and bursting with the freshest ingredients, including juicy tomatoes, feta cheese, capers, and olives, all locally grown. This recipe aims to capture the beauty of the flavors I fell in love with there. You can buy cooked ready-to-eat puy lentils in supermarkets—they are a great pantry standby and can be added to all kinds of soups.

Serves 4   calories 170   GF   (V/VE if using vegetable stock)

Carbs 15g   Sugar 7.5g   Protein 10g   Fiber 5.7g   Fat 6g   Sat Fat 3g   Salt 0.5g

1 medium onion, finely chopped
1 garlic clove, finely chopped
½ tablespoon olive oil
3 large zucchini
   (approx. 2¼ pounds),
   peeled and cubed
3 cups vegetable or chicken stock
½ cup feta cheese
¾ cup cooked puy lentils
4 pitted black olives, finely
   chopped
1½ teaspoons capers, coarsely
   chopped
8 cherry tomatoes, quartered

Sauté the onion and garlic in the olive oil and 1 tablespoon water for about 5 minutes until slightly softened. Add the zucchini and the stock, bring to a boil, reduce to a simmer, and cook for 15 to 20 minutes.

Remove from the heat, crumble the feta cheese into the stock, then blend until smooth. Return to the heat, add the cooked puy lentils, and bring back to a boil. Serve garnished with black olives, capers, and cherry tomatoes.

turkey and black quinoa with peas and basil

Just like chicken, turkey can be a little bland. But I like to see it as a blank canvas—something to enhance with the ingredients you add to it. Black quinoa has a wonderful nutty flavor and crunchy texture and, teamed with some fresh herbs, converts these meatballs into something truly special.

Serves 4

Carbs 15g   Sugar 3.8g   Protein 24g   Fiber 5g   Fat 6g   Sat Fat 1g   Salt 1g

⅓ cup black quinoa

9 ounces ground turkey

3 sprigs of thyme, leaves picked

2 sprigs of basil (about
    10 leaves), finely chopped

1 sprig of marjoram, leaves
    picked and finely chopped

1 scallion, finely chopped

1 tablespoon tomato paste

¾ teaspoon salt

½ teaspoon black pepper

1 tablespoon olive oil

4 cups chicken or vegetable stock

1¾ cups frozen peas

1 cup basil leaves, roughly torn

Place the quinoa in a strainer and rinse under cold water. Transfer to a small saucepan, cover with ⅔ cup water, add a pinch of salt, bring to a boil, and cook with the lid on for 10 to 12 minutes. Remove from the heat and leave undisturbed for 5 minutes so that the grains absorb any water left in the saucepan. Return to the strainer and run under cold water again to cool it completely. Squeeze out as much moisture as you can.

Mix the cooked quinoa with the turkey, thyme, basil, marjoram, scallion, tomato paste, salt, and pepper until everything is evenly combined. Shape the mixture into 20 meatballs, roughly ¾-ounce each or the size of a golf ball. Refrigerate for 10 minutes to solidify. This step can be done in advance, and the meatballs frozen, if desired.

Place a large heavy-bottomed frying pan or Dutch oven over medium heat with 1 tablespoon olive oil. Cook the meatballs on all sides until lightly browned, making sure not to burn them. Add the stock, bring to a boil, and simmer for 7 minutes. Add the peas and cook for another 3 minutes. Season to taste and stir in the basil just before serving.

watercress with balsamic beet-roast chickpeas and parsley crab

This is my staple watercress soup recipe, made all the more special by the addition of roasted chickpeas and decadent crab. This one is a show stopper!

Serves 4

Carbs 21g   Sugar 11g   Protein 18g   Fiber 7.5g   Fat 7g   Sat Fat 1g   Salt 0.7g

For the chickpeas
1 cup beet juice
1 tablespoon balsamic vinegar
1 x 14-ounce can chickpeas, drained, rinsed, and dried
salt and pepper

For the soup
½ small leek, finely chopped
1 garlic clove, chopped
1 celery rib, coarsely chopped
1 large zucchini (approx. 9 ounces), coarsely chopped
½ tablespoon olive oil
2¼ cups vegetable or chicken stock
3 sun-dried tomatoes
3½ ounces fresh white crabmeat
few sprigs of parsley or tarragon, finely chopped
squeeze of lemon juice
12 ounces watercress
1½ cups unsweetened soy milk

To make the chickpeas, place the beet juice and balsamic vinegar in a small saucepan and bring to a boil. Simmer for 20 to 25 minutes, until the liquid has reduced to about ¼ cup, and has a thick syrupy consistency.

Preheat the oven to 400°F. Place the chickpeas in a small baking pan and pour over half of the syrup, mixing well. Season and roast for 10 minutes. Remove from the oven, pour over the remaining syrup, and roast for another 10 to 15 minutes, keeping an eye to make sure the syrup does not burn. When ready, set aside.

Sauté the leek, garlic, celery, and zucchini in the olive oil and 1 tablespoon of water for about 5 to 8 minutes. Add a splash more water if necessary. Pour in the stock, then the sun-dried tomatoes. Bring to a boil and simmer for 15 minutes.

Mix the crabmeat with the chopped parsley or tarragon, then season with salt, pepper, and a squeeze of lemon juice. Refrigerate until needed.

Remove the sun-dried tomatoes then add the watercress and soy milk. Simmer for a couple of minutes to soften. Blend until smooth and season to taste. Serve, topped with a spoonful of crabmeat and a scattering of chickpeas.

superfood soups

This chapter champions known superfoods, and includes recipes jam-packed with ingredients such as avocado, spinach, chia seeds, quinoa, and coconut—all ingredients known to be particularly high in vitamins and antioxidants. It also looks at how a collection of ingredients can be combined into a dish that is truly powerful.

The Hangover Soup is inspired by a good, old-fashioned English breakfast; it takes the healthier, more nutritious elements and presents them in a rehydrating and comforting soup. The Purity Soup, as its name suggests, tastes and feels thoroughly pure, and is a fantastic detox. A soup for breakfast may seem strange, but the breakfast bowls in this chapter are anything but. Full of ingredients that give you long-lasting, slow-releasing energy, they are a great way to start the day. The beautifully tart Chilled Rhubarb, Orange, and Chia Seed Soup is served with a scoop of naturally sweetened Ginger and Vanilla Frozen Yogurt and makes a sophisticated and satisfying dessert.

These soups are designed to pack a nutritional punch—they are about as feel-good as food can be.

carrot, coconut, and ginger with cilantro sambal

Carrot and cilantro is a soup classic. Here, I have simply taken inspiration from the essence of these ingredients and presented it in a slightly different way. Coconuts are simple to crack open, but can also be bought already prepared in supermarkets.

Serves 4 calories 227 DF GF (V/VE if using vegetable stock)

Carbs 17.1g   Sugar 13.4g   Protein 3.1g   Fiber 10.9g   Fat 14g   Sat Fat 11g   Salt 0.2g

1¼ cups fresh coconut, grated
½ teaspoon cumin seeds
½ teaspoon coriander seeds
2 shallots, diced
1 garlic clove, coarsely chopped
5 tablespoons ginger, peeled
   and grated
½ teaspoon chile flakes
½ tablespoon coconut oil
1½ pounds carrots
3 cups vegetable or chicken stock

Cilantro Sambal
2 cups cilantro, coarsely chopped
⅓ cup grated fresh coconut
1 tablespoon ginger, peeled
   and grated
1 small green chile, seeded
   and coarsely chopped
juice of 1 lime
salt and pepper

If using a whole coconut, prepare it by piercing the three eyes with a skewer, and drain out the liquid. Then, wrap it in a towel, place on a hard surface, such as the floor (or take it outside), and give it a firm blow with a hammer to crack it open. Use a spoon to gently lift the flesh away from the harder exterior and remove the brown skin using a potato peeler if desired.

Toast the cumin and coriander seeds in a small frying pan for about 2 minutes, then grind in a mortar and pestle.

Sauté the shallots, garlic, ginger, chile flakes, and ground spices in the coconut oil and 1 tablespoon water for about 5 minutes, stirring occasionally. Add a splash of water if the mixture sticks to the pan.

Add the carrots, fresh coconut, and stock. Bring to a boil and simmer for 30 to 35 minutes until the carrots are soft.

To make the sambal, place the cilantro, grated coconut, ginger, and chile into a mini food processor and pulse to a coarse, dry paste. Stir in the lime juice and season to taste.

When the soup is ready, blend until smooth, season and serve topped with the sambal.

purity soup with citrus-cured salmon, avocado, pink grapefruit, and watercress

When I first made this soup, it occurred to me how pure it tasted, and so it acquired its name. The addition of fresh citrus flavors, creamy avocado, and peppery watercress make it deliciously refreshing too. You could serve the salmon garnish in little baby gem lettuce leaves instead if you wish. In summer months, this soup is excellent chilled and served with the garnish as a salad on the side. It doesn't retain its bright green color for very long, so best to serve it as soon as possible.

Serves 4 calories 225 DF GF

Carbs 16g   Sugar 13g   Protein 9g   Fiber 6g   Fat 12g   Sat Fat 3.5g   Salt 0.2g

For the salmon garnish
1 pink grapefruit, halved
juice of 1 lime, plus a little extra lime or lemon for the avocado
1 teaspoon agave syrup
3-ounce salmon fillet
½ ripe avocado, diced
small handful of watercress leaves

For the soup
1 small onion, coarsely chopped
3 tablespoons ginger, grated
2 garlic cloves, chopped
1 Granny Smith apple, cored and diced
½ tablespoon coconut oil

First, make the citrus-cured salmon: Squeeze the juice from one half of the grapefruit, combine with the lime juice in a small bowl, and whisk in the agave syrup. Slice the salmon into very thin strips and add to the curing juice. Make sure it's covered, and refrigerate for 30 minutes.

Remove the segments from the remaining grapefruit half as neatly as possible. Chop each segment into thirds. Dice the avocado half and dress with a little lime or lemon juice to preserve its color.

To make the soup, sauté the onion, ginger, garlic, and apple in the coconut oil and 1 tablespoon of water for 10 to 15 minutes over low heat, stirring regularly. Add a splash more water if necessary.

3¾ cups vegetable stock

5½ ounces kale, any tough stalks removed

3½ ounces spinach

1½ ripe avocados (use the leftover half from the garnish)

⅓ cup parsley

zest of 1 and juice of ½ lemon

Add the stock and bring to a boil before adding the kale, followed by the spinach. There will seem like a vast quantity of leaves for the amount of liquid used, but they will wilt very quickly. Encourage this by pressing them down with a spoon or spatula.

Simmer for 5 to 7 minutes. Remove from the heat and let cool a little, then add the avocado, parsley, lemon zest, and juice. Blend immediately to retain the vibrant color.

Divide the soup between four bowls. Pour off the curing juice and place the salmon on top of the soup, followed by the grapefruit, diced avocado, and some watercress leaves. Serve immediately.

hazelnut, cranberry, and chia seed oatcakes

These are a perfect accompaniment to soup and delicious spread with nut butter and topped with a few slices of banana to stave off any sweet cravings. The delicate sweetness from the cranberries makes them a tasty snack in their own right.

Makes 24

Carbs 5g   Sugar 0.8g   Protein 1.5g   Fiber 0.8g   Fat 2g   Sat Fat 0.2g   Salt 0.3g

⅓ cup blanched hazelnuts

1½ cups jumbo oats

½ teaspoon baking soda

1 teaspoon sea salt flakes

1 tablespoon hazelnut butter

½ cup boiling water

Preheat the oven to 300°F and line a baking sheet with parchment paper. Place the hazelnuts in a dry frying pan over medium heat and toast until golden brown. Let cool a little before chopping coarsely.

In a food processor, pulse-blend 1 cup of the jumbo oats, the baking soda, and salt to a fine powder. Add the

¼ cup dried cranberries,
coarsely chopped

1 teaspoon chia seeds

hazelnut butter and pulse a few times to incorporate.
Slowly add the water and stop mixing as soon as you have a
sticky paste. Finally, add the hazelnuts, dried cranberries,
chia seeds, and remaining jumbo oats and pulse a few
times until everything is just combined.

Transfer to a clean surface and gather the mixture together
into a firm ball. Place between two sheets of parchment
paper and roll out to ⅛-inch thickness. Remove the top
piece of parchment and cut out 24 oatcakes using a 2-inch
round cutter. Transfer to the lined baking sheet and bake
for 30 minutes until golden brown. Let cool on a wire rack.
They will keep for up to a week in an airtight container.

spinach, oat, and hazelnut milk soup

The oats are multifunctional in this recipe, imparting their goodness and creating a creamy consistency to thicken the soup. It may sound odd, but it works and is a clever way to introduce a slow-burning grain into a meal that is not just oatmeal. This soup is the most electrifying green color—almost too pretty to eat!

Serves 4   calories 131   DF V VE

Carbs 17.5g   Sugar 6g   Protein 4.5g   Fiber 4g   Fat 4g   Sat Fat 0.6g   Salt 0.5g

½ small leek, coarsely chopped
I celery rib, coarsely chopped
½ tablespoon olive oil
⅓ cup jumbo oats
2 cups vegetable or chicken stock
I4 ounces spinach, rinsed and drained
I cup hazelnut milk (soy or almond milk will also work)
I teaspoon freshly grated nutmeg
a handful of fresh basil
salt and pepper

Sauté the leek and celery in the olive oil and I tablespoon water for about 5 minutes, until softened. Stir in the oats, followed by the stock. Bring to a boil and simmer for 5 minutes. Add the spinach; if you are using a large saucepan, all the spinach may fit, otherwise add it in batches, allowing each batch to wilt before adding more.

Simmer for a couple of minutes to soften the spinach slightly. Add the hazelnut milk, nutmeg, and basil. Blend until smooth (a high-powered blender works best here). Season to taste, adding a touch more nutmeg if necessary. Bring to just below boiling point before serving.

Serve with Hazelnut, Cranberry, and Chia Seed Oatcakes (page I35).

eat-the-rainbow vegetable broth

Serving these wonderful ingredients virtually uncooked preserves all of their natural goodness, vibrant color, and texture. The name comes from its colorful appearance, and falls in line with many health recommendations suggesting that our diet includes fruits and vegetables that, quite literally, resemble the colors of the rainbow.

Serves 4

Carbs 26g   Sugar 11g   Protein 19g   Fiber 7g   Fat 4g   Sat Fat 0.8g   Salt 0.5g

½ cup mixed wild rice (I use
   red and wild rice)
⅓ cup Turmeric and Lemongrass
   Paste (page 18)
2 cups coconut water
½ cup edamame
1 cup shiitake mushrooms,
   or 4 medium mushrooms
   (1 per bowl)
2 cups purple sprouting
   broccoli, chopped
2 medium carrots, julienned
2 scallions, finely sliced
4 small radishes, finely sliced
1 tablespoon nori, finely sliced
5½ ounces fresh tuna, thinly
   sliced
1 tablespoon black sesame seeds

Cook the rice according to package instructions. When ready, strain, run under cold water to stop the cooking process, and set aside.

Gently sauté the turmeric and lemongrass paste over low heat to release all the flavor. Add the coconut water, along with 3¾ cups water, and bring to a boil. Simmer for 15 minutes. When ready, pass through a muslin-lined strainer (or use a clean cheesecloth) and return to a clean saucepan. Season to taste and bring to a gentle simmer.

Add all the vegetables, cooking just long enough to heat them through, about 2 to 3 minutes.

Place the rice in the bowls, then cover with the broth and vegetables. Top with the nori, fresh tuna, and sesame seeds and serve immediately.

the hangover soup

This soup does for a hangover what chicken soup does for the common cold. Marmite and Worcestershire sauce add salty notes while Tobasco sauce introduces some spice to cleanse from the inside out. Rehydrating, comforting, and nutritious—a whole new kind of cure!

Serves 4

Carbs 17.7g   Sugar 6.8g   Protein 10g   Fiber 7.7g   Fat 1.5g   Sat Fat 0.4g   Salt 1.7g

2½ cups cherry tomatoes
I tablespoon Tabasco sauce,
   plus extra to serve
I small onion, halved and
   thinly sliced
I garlic clove, finely chopped
3 tablespoons Worcestershire
   sauce
2 to 3 cups portobello
   mushrooms, coarsely chopped
3 cups beef stock (or use
   Mushroom Stock, page 16,
   to make vegetarian)
I x 14-ounce can navy beans,
   drained and rinsed
I teaspoon Marmite
small bunch of parsley,
   coarsely chopped
salt and pepper

Preheat the oven to 475°F. Place half of the cherry tomatoes in a small roasting dish with the Tabasco sauce, a pinch of salt, and a generous grinding of pepper. Roast for 15 minutes.

Sauté the onion and garlic over low heat in I tablespoon of Worcestershire sauce and 2 tablespoons water, stirring regularly to prevent them from sticking and burning. Add more water if necessary. After about 10 minutes, when nicely browned and caramelized, add the mushrooms and remaining tomatoes and cook for another 3 to 4 minutes. Add the stock and navy beans, bring to a boil, and cook for 15 to 20 minutes.

Season with the remaining Worcestershire sauce and the Marmite, and pepper if needed. Serve topped with the Tabasco-roasted tomatoes, some chopped parsley, and Tabasco sauce on the side for an added kick!

superfood chowder

Soy milk has a beautiful, delicate flavor, and makes this soup rich and creamy without being overly calorific. It also boasts a whole array of benefits, being rich in omega-3 and 6 and high in protein and fiber, essential fatty acids, vitamins, and minerals. Furthermore, it contains mostly unsaturated fat with zero cholesterol. A worthwhile addition to any diet!

Serves 4 calories 241 DF GF

. . . .

Carbs 22.5g   Sugar 7g   Protein 22g   Fiber 4.6g   Fat 6g   Sat Fat 0.8g   Salt 1.1g

. . . .

⅓ cup black quinoa

pinch of salt

1½ cups unsweetened soy milk

9 ounces smoked haddock

1 bay leaf

1 onion, peeled and halved

6 peppercorns

1 medium leek, finely sliced

1 garlic clove, chopped

½ tablespoon olive oil

1 fresh corn on the cob

3 cups vegetable stock

5½ ounces spinach,
 finely shredded

3 tablespoons chives,
 finely chopped

Place the quinoa in a strainer and rinse under cold water. Transfer to a small saucepan, cover with ⅔ cup water, add a pinch of salt, bring to a boil, and cook with the lid on for 10 minutes. Remove from the heat and leave undisturbed for 5 minutes, so that the grains absorb any remaining water. Return to the strainer and run under cold water again to cool completely. Set aside until needed.

Place the soy milk in a medium saucepan with the smoked haddock, bay leaf, onion halves, and peppercorns. Slowly bring to a boil and simmer for 3 minutes. Remove from the heat and let stand, covered, for 5 minutes. Strain and set the cooking broth aside.

Clean the saucepan and return to the heat. Sauté the leek and garlic in the oil and 1 tablespoon water over low heat for about 5 minutes, until soft and translucent. Stand the corn upright and slide the blade of a sharp knife along the length of the cob, removing the kernels as you do so. Add these to the saucepan, along with the reserved cooking broth and vegetable stock. Add the cob for added flavor. Bring to a boil, immediately reduce to a simmer, and cook for 7 to 10 minutes. When ready, remove the cobs and use a slotted spoon to skim any foam that has formed on the surface.

Add the cooked quinoa, along with the spinach and fish. Bring to just below boiling point, season to taste, garnish with some chopped chives, and serve immediately.

spiced root vegetable soup

This bejeweled soup belongs in the center of a table, shared by family and friends. Many of the spices used are known for their metabolism- and immunity-boosting properties. If you are serving up a feast, I recommend throwing together some Buckwheat Tortillas (pages 99–100). A loaf of Pumpkin Seed and Prune Rye Soda Bread (page 32) would be good to mop up the juices and some Vegetable Chips (pages 45–47) would be delicious.

Serves 6    (if using vegetable stock)

Carbs 22g   Sugar 11g   Protein 3.5g   Fiber 6g   Fat 2g   Sat Fat 0.3g   Salt 0.2g

1 red onion, sliced

1 garlic clove, finely chopped

2 medium carrots, peeled and
cut into ¾-inch cubes

½ tablespoon olive oil

¼ teaspoon chile flakes
(optional)

¼ teaspoon cayenne pepper

¼ teaspoon turmeric

½ teaspoon cinnamon

¾ teaspoon ground ginger

¾ teaspoon garam masala

1 medium sweet potato, peeled
and cut into ¾-inch cubes

1 large parsnip, peeled and cut
into ¾-inch cubes

5 cups vegetable or chicken stock

9 ounces vacuum-packed cooked
beets, cut into ¾-inch cubes,
juice reserved

3½ ounces baby spinach,
finely shredded

2 cups cilantro, torn

salt and pepper

Sauté the onion, garlic, and carrots in the olive oil and 1 tablespoon water for about 5 to 8 minutes, until the onion is soft. Add the spices, mix well, and cook for a minute or so. Add the sweet potato, parsnip, and stock. Bring to a boil and simmer for 20 minutes. Don't be tempted to allow the soup to simmer untimed or unwatched. It is important to cook the vegetables until they are just tender, otherwise they will fall apart.

Add the beet, its juice, and the spinach. Taste for seasoning, and stir through the cilantro just before serving. Alternatively, you could pile the cilantro on top of the soup if serving to a table of guests to create a bit of drama!

chilled avocado and wasabi with black sesame seed and nori booster

This recipe is quite rich, so a little goes a long way. To introduce some texture, serve topped with fresh slices of raw or seared tuna or even try a ceviche, curing some raw tuna in a little lime juice, salt, and pepper, and serving it atop some Hoisin Sesame Seed Wonton Crisps (page 58).

Serves 4

calories 274 DF GF V VE

Carbs 7.5g   Sugar 5g   Protein 7g   Fiber 6g   Fat 23g   Sat Fat 6g   Salt 0.2g

For the black sesame seed and nori booster
1 sheet nori
1 tablespoon black sesame seeds

For the soup
2 shallots, coarsely chopped
2 garlic cloves, coarsely chopped
2½ tablespoons ginger, peeled and coarsely chopped
1 teaspoon coconut oil
3 medium ripe avocados (approx. 2½ cups when prepared)
juice of 2 limes
7 ounces silken tofu
2 teaspoons wasabi paste
1 teaspoon white pepper
generous pinch of salt
1¼ cups coconut water

Preheat the oven to 400°F and place the nori on a baking sheet. Bake for 5 minutes until curled and crisp—it burns quickly, so keep an eye on it. Let cool, then pulse into small flakes. Add the sesame seeds and set aside.

Sauté the shallots, garlic, and ginger in the coconut oil and 1 tablespoon water for 5 minutes, until softened. Be sure they don't stick and burn.

Slice the avocados in half, remove the pit, and scoop out the flesh. Dress with a little lime juice to prevent it from browning. Transfer to a blender along with the tofu, wasabi, lime juice, white pepper, and salt. Add the sautéed onions, garlic, and ginger, along with the coconut water, and blend until smooth.

Chill in the fridge for a couple of hours and serve garnished with a sprinkling of the black sesame seed and nori booster.

Note: this soup is best eaten on the day it is made, as it doesn't keep its beautiful pastel green color or fresh flavors for long.

Not suitable for freezing

black rice, banana, and coconut breakfast bowl

Black rice has high levels of fiber, meaning it is absorbed at a slower rate into the body, keeping you feeling fuller for longer. Rarely would we be making breakfast for four, so this recipe serves two. If you are cooking for one, it will keep in the fridge until the following morning.

Serves 2

Carbs 50g   Sugar 16g   Protein 4.5g   Fiber 1.7g   Fat 4g   Sat Fat 3g   Salt 0.4g

½ cup black glutinous rice
½ teaspoon cinnamon
¼ teaspoon ground ginger
I slice fresh ginger
I cup coconut water
I banana, sliced, or other fruit
 of your choice
2½ tablespoons pomegranate
 seeds (optional)
½ cup unsweetened fresh
 almond milk
2 tablespoons coconut milk
a few mint leaves, to garnish

Soak the rice overnight. When ready to cook, rinse thoroughly, transfer to a small saucepan with the spices, ginger, coconut water, and ½ cup cold water. Bring to a boil, cover with a tight-fitting lid or foil, and simmer for 30 to 35 minutes.

Prepare the banana and pomegranate seeds. When the rice is cooked, add the almond milk and bring back to a boil. Simmer for a couple of minutes, then remove the ginger. Divide between two bowls and top with fruit and coconut milk. Garnish with mint leaves and serve.

Not suitable for freezing

A note on black glutinous rice

This is the unprocessed whole grain of traditional sticky white rice. Nutty in flavor, chewy in texture, and a vibrant burgundy color when cooked, it is high in fiber, iron, copper, zinc, and carotene, and packed with powerful antioxidants. It is lower in calories and carbohydrate than white and brown rice, and higher in protein. Take a look for it in your supermarket, but you are more likely to find it in health-food stores and online.

chilled rhubarb, orange, and chia seed soup

I have done little here to mask the beautiful tart flavors of rhubarb. Just a touch of agave syrup for sweetening, although roasting also helps to concentrate the natural sugars. Chia seeds are rich in omega-3 and high in protein and iron, making them a great little pantry standby. This soup is as decadent a dessert as any.

Serves 4   calories 47   GF   V

Carbs 6g   Sugar 5g   Protein 1.7g   Fiber 3.3g   Fat 0.9g   Sat Fat 0.1g   Salt 0g

For the consommé

1¼ pounds fresh pink rhubarb, cut into ¾-inch cubes
zest and juice of ½ orange
1 star anise
seeds of ½ vanilla bean (reserve other half for Ginger and Vanilla Frozen Yogurt on page 152)
1 tablespoon agave syrup or honey
1 bay leaf
2 teaspoons chia seeds
Ginger and Vanilla Frozen Yogurt, to serve
mint leaves, to garnish (optional)

Preheat the oven to 350°F and place the rhubarb, orange zest and juice, star anise, vanilla seeds and bean, agave syrup, bay leaf, and ⅔ cup water into a shallow roasting pan. Cook for 30 minutes, until the rhubarb is soft and breaks up easily. Let cool, remove the aromatics, and then use the back of a soup ladle to press as much of the rhubarb as possible through a strainer. You should have about ½ cup rhubarb pulp left over—set this aside to make the ginger and vanilla frozen yogurt.

Give the soup a little whisk and chill for 2 to 3 hours, or overnight. This can all be done a day ahead and can be frozen if you are using a glut of rhubarb from the garden.

When ready to serve, stir 1 teaspoon chia seeds through the soup and divide between four bowls. Top with a scoop of ginger andvanilla frozen yogurt, garnish with the remaining chia seeds, and a few small mint leaves if you have them.

Tip: It is nice to serve this soup in shallow glasses that have been cooling in the freezer.

ginger and vanilla frozen yogurt

This frozen yogurt is totally free from added sugar, gaining its sweetness from succulent golden raisins. The fresh ginger cuts through the creamy yogurt and the vanilla brings the whole thing together to produce a decadent dessert. This recipe makes a small quantity, but it is easy to double up if you want to make more.

Serves 4

Carbs 9g   Sugar 8.5g   Protein 3g   Fiber 0.8g   Fat 4g   Sat Fat 2.5g   Salt 0g

¼ cup golden raisins

¾ cup full-fat Greek yogurt

2½ tablespoons ginger, peeled and very finely grated

½ cup rhubarb pulp (see page 151)

seeds of ½ vanilla bean (reserved from Chilled Rhubarb Soup on page 151)

Place the golden raisins in a small saucepan and cover with ¼ cup of water. Bring to a boil and simmer for about 5 minutes. Take off the heat, let cool, and then blend to a smooth puree.

Add the Greek yogurt, ginger, rhubarb pulp, and vanilla seeds and blend for a few second more until nice and smooth.

Place in a small plastic tub and freeze. After a couple of hours, blend the frozen yogurt in a small food processor to remove any ice crystals, then return to the freezer. Repeat once more after another 2 hours. When ready to serve, let stand at room temperature for 10 to 15 minutes to allow it to soften slightly.

breakfast oat smoothie bowl done two ways

These two recipes are based on the idea of a smoothie, but made a lot more substantial by the addition of some beautiful garnishes that transform it into the kind of breakfast that will start your day off right. Hugely adaptable depending on what fruit you may have in your fridge, and what nutty seedy garnishes you have access to, these recipes are very much open to interpretation.

Blackberry Oat Smoothie Bowl with Berry, Seed, and Lime Zest Garnish

Serves 2

Carbs 46g   Sugar 26g   Protein 8g   Fiber 10g   Fat 7g   Sat Fat 0.9g   Salt 0.2g

½ cup jumbo oats, I tablespoon
   set aside for toasting
½ tablespoon chia seeds
2 small bananas
I cup frozen blackberries, or fresh
   with 4 ice cubes
2 pitted soft prunes
½ tablespoons fresh ginger, grated
I cup unsweetened almond or soy milk
pinch of cinnamon

For the garnish
¼ cup raspberries
3 tablespoons blueberries
3 tablespoons blackberries
½ tablespoon golden flaxseeds
I tablespoon pumpkin seeds
lime zest

Place the oats (minus I tablespoon), chia seeds, banana, blackberries, prunes, ginger, and almond or soy milk in a blender and process until smooth. Toast the remaining jumbo oats in a dry frying pan over medium heat until golden. Dust with a pinch of cinnamon and set aside.

Divide soup between two bowls and serve garnished with the berries, seeds, toasted oats, and a sprinkling of lime zest.

Mango, Tofu, and Coconut Oat Smoothie Bowl with Chia Seeds, Kiwi, and Passion Fruit

Serves 2   calories 264   DF   V   VE

Carbs 42g   Sugar 26g   Protein 8.5g   Fiber 8g   Fat 5g   Sat Fat 0.9g   Salt 0.2g

½ cup jumbo oats
1 medium mango, peeled (approx.
   9 ounces prepared weight)
3½ ounces silken tofu
¼ teaspoon ground turmeric
1 tablespoon fresh ginger, peeled and grated
½ tablespoon agave syrup
¾ cup coconut water
zest of ½ and juice of 1 lime
4 ice cubes
1 kiwi, peeled and sliced
1 passion fruit, seeds scraped out
½ tablespoon chia seeds
1 sprig of mint

Place the oats, three quarters of the mango, the tofu, turmeric, ginger, agave syrup, coconut water, lime zest, and juice in a blender with the ice cubes and process until smooth.

Serve garnished with the remaining mango, kiwi, passion fruit, chia seeds, and mint.

Not suitable for freezing

suppliers

Living in central London, I am surrounded by stores selling almost every ingredient I could possibly imagine. However, coming from a small town in Ireland, I am aware that unusual ingredients are not always that easy to find. Wherever you live, the internet is the perfect solution and can easily become your local supermarket. I use it a lot for buying pantry, Asian, and other unusual ingredients, and for the odd online grocery shop when I am strapped for time. However, nothing can replace being able to see, touch, and smell fresh ingredients, so I would always recommend buying fruit, vegetables, meat, and fish from your local stores.

Asian ingredients

These suppliers sell a wide variety of Asian ingredients, including miso pastes, tofu, bonito flakes, and kombu for Japanese dashi, gochujang, nori, and konnyaki shirataki noodles:

www.asianfoodgrocer.com

www.koamart.com

www.importfood.com

Spices

www.spicesinc.com

www.penzeys.com

www.thespicehouse.com

www.mountainroseherbs.com

Mexican

You will find ancho chiles here, as well as cooked hominy in cans.

www.mexgrocer.com

www.thechileguy.com

Online grocery shopping

Many of the unusual ingredients in this book can be found on iGourmet, so it is worth checking it out:

www.igourmet.com

Pantry essentials

These websites are fantastic for grains, pulses, flours, and oils, among other things:

www.amazon.com

www.bobsredmill.com

index

acknowledgments

Writing a cookbook has been a dream of mine for a very long time and the reality came about as a result of much support, encouragement, and belief from my family, friends, and people I have been very lucky to encounter along the way.

To my Mum, and Dad who is sadly no longer alive, thank you for encouraging me to explore my passion for cooking—even though you had just put me through four years of fashion college. Mum, thank you for all the endless hours we spend on the phone, for your infinite wisdom and advice. My brothers Mark and Gary, sisters Liz and Grace, thank you for always believing in me.

There were many tasters employed to help me develop the recipes in this book. Kate, Ciara, and Freda, the team at Propeller, my family, my husband and his gorgeous family, thank you all for lending me your tastebuds. There were two in particular, whose help and never-ending love of soup helped me to refine many of the recipes in this book. Mikey and Sammy, I love you for loving soup as much as you do and for being such wonderful friends.

My journey from kitchens and managing bakeries to food styling came about because a very special lady, Annie Rigg, took a chance on me after I pestered her with numerous emails asking her to give me a job. I have spent many happy years assisting Annie (and walking Mungo) and she has taught me everything I know. You are inspiration personified and a cherished friend.

An incredible team of people have worked on this book. Liz Belton, I was blown away by the props you chose—I couldn't have loved them more. Laura Edwards, as always your talent is insurmountable. Annie Rigg, your magic touch flows through each and every page. Louise Leffler you have brought it all together to create a book I feel so proud to be a part of. I cannot thank you all enough for bringing my ideas to life.

I feel incredibly lucky and honored to be writing my first book for Kyle Books, such an esteemed publishing house. A million thank you's for giving me this opportunity. A big thank you also to Claire, my editor. You have been endlessly patient and helpful—I have so enjoyed our journey together.

To my little daughter Elsie. Thank you for being the angel you are and bouncing happily in your bouncer while I finished this book.

And finally, to Rich, my husband and best friend—you are the most amazing person I have ever met. I am so lucky to have you. Thank you for loving me, even though I made you eat soup for six months!